Helping Your Aging Parents

A GUIDE FOR CAREGIVERS WITH PRACTICAL TIPS TO TAKE CARE OF YOUR LOVED ONES, STAY ORGANIZED, AND MAINTAIN BALANCE IN YOUR LIFE

JOHN FAGAN MD

JEANINE FAGAN MBA

CLADDAGHPUBLISHING

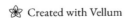

Table of Contents

Dedication   7
Introduction   9

1. WHAT'S HAPPENING TO MY LOVED ONE?   13
   The Doctor is in.

   Skin   15
   Musculoskeletal   16
   Arthritic changes   16
   Gastrointestinal   16
   Heart and Lungs   17
   Bladder   17
   Brain changes   18
   Feet   20
   Hearing   20
   Vision   21
   Immune System   22
   Medical Visits   22

2. HOW DO WE AVOID OR MINIMIZE THE
   CONSEQUENCES OF AGING?   24
   Fountain of Youth

   Proper diet   24
   Exercise   25
   Avoid Alcohol and Smoking   26
   Work that Brain   26
   Laugh   27

3. TALKING ABOUT AGING WITH YOUR
   LOVED ONE.   29
   The Other Talk

   The Conversation   30
   Get Ready   32
   Get Set   33
   Go!   35

Keep Going   37
Practical applications to apply as soon as possible   41

4. ASSESS THE SITUATION AND TAKE ACTION.   43
    Aging in Place
Bathroom   44
Stay home   46
Home Cleaning   47
Financial Creativeness   48
Brighten Their Surroundings   48
Staying in Touch   50
To Drive or Not To Drive   51
Telephone   54
Internet   54
Financial Accounts   55
Credit cards   56
Paying Medical Bills   56
Declining mental function and the chaos it can cause   57
It's about you too   57

Untitled   59

5. CHOICES AND DECISIONS.   60
    Prioritize
In-Home Care   60
Finding the Right In-home Care Provider   61
What is the difference between Independent and
Assisted Living?   62
The Village Concept   66
Continuing Care Retirement Community (CCRC)
and Life Care Communities (LCC)   67
Nursing Home/Skilled Nursing Facility   67
Where Do You Go From Here?   68
How To Find The Right Place   69
How Much Care Do Your Parents Need?   71
Understand the Key Differences Between In-Home
Care and Assisted Living   71
Understand the Financial Situation   73
Is it time for Assisted Living?   75
What Else Is Critical to Know?   76

6. BEING A HEALTH ADVOCATE.   80
Medical Care for Your Loved One
What else can you do to ensure your loved one's care?   86

7. TAKING CARE OF THE CAREGIVER.   88
Me or you? Push-pull!

8. THE FINAL CHAPTER   98
Letting go while you hold on
Palliative versus Hospice   98
End-of-Life Planning, Hospice, and Bereavement
Information   99
When is it time to look into hospice services?   100

9. PREPARING YOUR LOVED ONE AND
YOURSELF FOR THE INEVITABLE: 103
Getting ready to say goodbye
The dying process   105
Grief is part of letting go   107
Taking care of yourself after a loved one has died   108

Conclusion   111
Untitled   113
The Caregivers Binder   115
Resources   117
About the Authors   119

Dedication

To Dad, Peggy, and Caitlin who have provided us with the love and forgiveness to help us learn to be selfless on our journey of caregiving.

Introduction

"Right there, a part of me died, and I knew I was going to have to change," anguished Sharon upon realizing her precious mother could no longer be left alone in the kitchen. She had set a frying pan of hot oil on fire... for the third time.

"By the time I got to my parents' home, and I only live six blocks from them, flames were licking at the underside of their cabinets over the stove. My dad couldn't figure out how to make the fire extinguisher work. And, worse, my mother seemed confused about *why* the pan had caught on fire."

Life as Sharon knew it changed...not about to change or was going to change, but it had already changed. She was no longer the child; she had become the parent to her parents. The dynamics had been inching toward that direction for several years. She had tried pointing that out to her sisters, but they were unwilling or unable to acknowledge the changes in their parents. In many ways, it was convenient for them to ignore their parents' transition from being in charge people to needing care. Sharon's sisters didn't see the day-to-day changes in their parents' lives because the sisters lived hours away and did not see their parents frequently.

Sharon and her sisters had talked to both parents several years earlier about moving to an independent or assisted living facility. Understandably they were adamant they were not, repeat, were not going to be moving into "an old folks' home." They didn't want to discuss options for aging in place. Why? Because if you don't acknowledge something, it doesn't exist.

Sharon was the one her dad called four to six times a day when he wanted or needed something. She strongly suspected it was just his way of trying to stay in control because he had an inkling his wife was starting to have problems and was scared.

Listening to the distress in Sharon's voice made us realize how important it is for families to have easy-to-understand guides without a lot of medical and legal jargon compounding and confusing the many questions family members must confront about aging parents.

What to do about aging in place? Hint: it's not just about having your parents physically safe in their home.

What to do about moving them to an independent or assisted living facility? Hint: due diligence is of critical importance.

What to do if they are hospitalized, and medical staff informs you that the time has arrived to prepare for the end? Do your parents require visiting nurses, caregivers, or hospice? Do you know your parents' last wishes? Having a conversation about what your parent wants is not an easy discussion. We find it hard to talk about our mortality.

These are just a few of the many questions that should and need to be answered BEFORE your parents get into a critical situation where they can't make their wishes known. The questions are not *how* questions; they are *what* questions. *How* questions can keep family members stuck in an endless loop of questions without ever moving forward. They get bogged down in the details. *What* questions are proactive and keep all of your parents' wishes and desires moving forward toward a logical solution.

This book will help you understand what your parents are going through from both the adult childs' and the aging parents' perspectives. Once you see things from different sides, it can help ease the pain, the burden, and, perhaps, even the guilt of the final leg of your parents' journey. Who are the Fagans, and why should you listen to them on this personal and complex issue facing your loved ones or elderly parents?

Dr. John Fagan is a board-certified Geriatric and Family physician with over 35 years in private and group practice. As the medical director of Casa Colina's Geriatric assessment center in Los Angeles County, California, Dr. Fagan has experienced family caregiving complexities from all angles. He understands the family, the patient, and the difficulties of juggling all the responsibilities as a loved one ages. Jeanine Fagan spent her career working with pharmaceutical companies, where she learned the clinical side of treatments and the equally important side of how treatments affect patients and families. Jeanine also spent time in the hospice field, where she witnessed first-hand the problems arising as parents age or loved ones require additional living assistance. Mrs. Fagan is a fierce patient advocate. She has seen when life-saving treatments did not work for a parent. She has watched families financially ruined because of poor decisions while a loved one was battling a terminal illness. Jeanine has seen the anxiety experienced by families as they grapple with the end-of-life questions and fears.

Dr. Fagan and Jeanine are passionate about helping other families handle the "aging journey" with ease and love. Between the years of medical knowledge and the personal journey of caregiving for their parents and grandparents, Dr. and Mrs. Fagan are a dynamic source of empowerment for others with aging parents.

Real-life examples are included. It is important to see how others managed caregiving for their aging parents. The Fagans will provide you with practical solutions to real-life caregiving and aging problems. The resources section includes added guidelines and templates to help you start organizing for this new venture. Caregiving can be challenging, but if you are prepared, you will find that there is nobody better equipped to care for a loved one. You have been chosen!

"In the circle of life
it's the wheel of fortune
it's the leap of faith
it's the band of hope
till we find our place"
Lion King Circle of Life

CHAPTER 1

What's happening to my loved one?

THE DOCTOR IS IN.

M y elderly mother leaned forward on the sofa to hear me. I could tell she was straining to make sense of what I was saying. It's not that she had Alzheimer's or dementia. No, it was simply because she needed hearing aids. Something that would significantly increase her quality of life, yet she was reluctant to do so.

There can be a few reasons she was reluctant to get hearing aids. It could be financial, vanity, or even fear. Financial fears often present themselves in seniors. Prices continue to climb, and our seniors are on fixed budgets. Hearing aids are not usually covered by insurance, and they are expensive. The technology continues to evolve, requiring hearing aids to be updated. It could be a fear of admitting her body is changing or possibly that her social group would judge her. Many seniors have difficulty recognizing that the body is starting to fail, and you, as the caregiver, must be empathetic but honest.

It's challenging to acknowledge the struggles aging parents are going through because they often don't want to talk about it to their children. Many aging parents don't want to be a burden to their children, and thus, they don't like to discuss the aging process. Some, particularly men, feel like they have failed, even though the aging process is natural.

We prepare for the birth and parenting of our children, but we often overlook what is needed for the caregiving and death of our aging parents. By being prepared, many of the aging problems can be navigated calmly and will be less stressful for our elderly parents and the families caring for them. Approaching this time in our parents' lives with a sense of being prepared will also help ease the burden

According to the U.S. Department of Health and Human Services, seventy percent, yes, 70%, of people over the age of 65 will need some type of long-term care support, whether help from their children or another caregiver. Those numbers can be staggering.

Let's put it into perspective. In 2019, 54.1 million people were aged 65 and older (up from 39.6 million in 2009). This demographic is projected to reach 80.8 million by 2040 and 94.7 million by 2060. Today, only a tiny percentage of American seniors and disabled people live in institutional settings. Both populations are growing, and older Americans are one of the fastest-growing demographics in the country. In 2019, the 65-74 age group (31.5 million) was more than 14 times larger than in 1900 (2.19 million); the 75-84 group (16 million) was 20 times larger, and the 85+ group (6.6 million) was more than 53 times larger than it was in 1900.

Here's the kicker, less than 50% of adults under 60 have discussed long-term care or retirement with their parents. Statistics and percentages are great information, but what does this mean to you?

Let's get personal. Your mom will typically live three to four years longer than your dad/her husband. If longevity runs in your family, it can be much longer. Your parents or step-parents may not need long-term care support, but overall, approximately one in five people over 65 will need it for five years or longer.

In the case of Sharon and her parents, long life runs on both sides of the family; typically, the women live to be 94-96. Her dad has already outlived his family members by 25 years. Sharons' mom is now 95 and her dad 96 years old. As the oldest child, Sharon moved back to the small town she grew up in to help care for her aging parents. Somewhat annoyed about the constant complaints of her father, she reached out to Dr. John Fagan, a board-certified Geriatric physician, for an explanation of what was going on with her parents in terms of their aging. Dr. Fagan explained to Sharon that her parents were not being cranky or trying to annoy her. Physical changes occur at the molecular and cellular levels, causing seniors to act or behave in specific ways.

He explained the aging process by going over the major areas of the body: skin, hearing, vision, muscles, reproductive organs, gastrointestinal, cardiac, lungs, bladder, neurologic, feet, and immune system. Understanding what your parents are going through with the aging process gives you a better insight as to the reason(s) why they're acting as they do. Keep in mind this doesn't explain everything, due to individual personalities. Still, it does help to provide a different perspective; perhaps a gentler or more empathetic ear is called for when listening to them. Remember, they may not consider what they're telling you as complaining. They may think of it as trying to explain what they're feeling.

This explanation helped Sharon better understand her dad, knowing there were actual physical reasons for him telling her about how he was feeling. With this understanding, Sharon began to work on herself. Adult relationships require letting go and working on oneself. You can't change other people, but you can try to understand the reasons behind their actions. Sharon admitted that she still viewed him as complaining but agreed she would work on her attitude by learning as much as possible about the aging process. Each organ goes through visible and invisible changes as the human body ages. While the exterior body is how we witness aging, we know changes occur in all organ systems.

SKIN

When people age, usually by the late 60s, they lose the layer of fat just underneath the skin. The largest organ of our human body, the skin, is where some temperature regulation occurs. This explains why older folks often have difficulty controlling their body temperature. You may have noticed grandma always had a shawl wrapped around her shoulders, or maybe even you are starting to wear sweaters when you used to enjoy short sleeves.

Your dad may constantly be wrapping his arms after activities. You learn that he's scraped his skin and is bleeding, although what you witnessed seemed like a gentle bump of his arm against the table. How could such a bump have ripped off his skin, you wonder? As aging occurs, the skin also becomes thinner. This thin skin can tear very easily, causing bleeds under the skin, especially on the forearms. You may see dark purple spots on the torn skin.

MUSCULOSKELETAL

While some older folks are still out there pumping iron/weights, most of us gradually start losing lean muscle mass, which is replaced with fat. Women, more than men, tend toward decreased bone density, which can lead to osteoporosis and increased risk of fracture. Another factor for reduced bone density in women is the ovaries fail or stop working. The hormone needed to maintain bone density, estrogen, diminishes.

This leads to further hormonal issues. Decreased hormones can cause vasomotor symptoms (hot flashes) and atrophy of the vagina and urethra. For men, testosterone production should continue, but there is a slightly increased risk of developing reduced testosterone, which can cause fatigue and lack of motivation.

ARTHRITIC CHANGES

How often have you heard your mom or dad say their joints hurt? It makes sense because we use our joints all of the time. A gradual inflammation of the joints due to wear and tear leads to calcium buildup, causing osteoarthritis as aging occurs. Arthritic changes occur in most joints of the body, but you may see it first in the fingers and the base of the thumb. The knees, hips, and feet are also often affected.

GASTROINTESTINAL

Many older people complain about being constipated. Often constipation results from a diet low in fiber or one low in fluids. Medications can also cause constipation as well as a sedentary lifestyle. If your parents take an opioid it is important to take some kind of laxative. Dr. Fagan recommends taking one with the dual action of stool softener and laxative.

Constipation can be challenging if one or both parents don't want to change their diet. Traditionally, it's been the female in charge of meal preparation, and if she's reluctant to change what and how she's cooking or if her spouse refuses to eat more fiber, the caregiver may feel helpless. Trying to convince her parents that they needed more fiber in their diet became a real headache for Sharon. Dad would not eat what mom would prepare. Sharon got creative and introduced her dad to fiber bars. There are lots of ways to increase fiber, but natural fruits and vegetables still remain the healthiest option.

HEART AND LUNGS

Just because a parent is aging does not mean they will automatically have heart disease. With age, plaque can build up in the arteries. Dangerous levels are usually related to smoking and poor diet. Discussing the possibilities of genetic heart conditions and lifestyle with physicians is essential. Doctors can do many tests to assess the aging circulatory system. This screening should start in your 50's, so caregivers pay attention.

Other friends of Sharon talked about some of the more subtle changes they saw in their parents. Darla noticed that her mom shopping in the grocery store seemed to run out of breath a little more often than she had in the past. Her mother shrugged it off, but Darla called the doctor to determine if she should be concerned. As Dr. Fagan explains, there is a gradual decrease in lung function with decreased ability to inhale as a person ages. Also, the airways tend to be less robust as they exhale. This can lead to mild lung disease. More serious problems are usually caused by smoking and exposure to environmental/ infectious causes.

BLADDER

As we become older, the bladder becomes weaker. A weak bladder causes a reduction in the strength of the urine stream. Women can have laxity in the ligaments holding the bladder and vagina. Weakness of the ligaments leads to a change in the angle of the urethra which can cause leakage of urine with increased abdominal pressure such as coughing or sneezing. This is called stress incontinence. As the bladder ages, the muscle can become weak leading to incomplete emptying. This can cause incontinence if there is too much urine in the bladder called overflow incontinence. For men, the prostate is a gland surrounding the base of the bladder and the urethra. This gland gradually enlarges over time and can block the flow of urine. For both men and women, the bladder often becomes more active, contracting on its own, causing decreased time for urination. This is called urge incontinence or overactive bladder. All of these factors lead to a higher incidence of incontinence of urination for both men and women.

Sharon's mother was embarrassed to go to the restroom so frequently, and it often took a while for her to do her business. She repeatedly apologized, mainly when they went to restaurants or social gatherings—understanding the physical "why" helped Sharon to be more patient with both of her parents when they needed to go to the bathroom, often twice in the same meal. They weren't doing it because they wanted to; it is simply a part of aging.

Technology is challenging for many, especially for and parents. Recall spending days in the library researching topics. Do you remember the door-to-door encyclopedia salesman? Having a set of encyclopedias was the way many of us found answers to pressing questions. Our parents probably never learned how to "google" or ask "Siri" for the answer, so things we think are simple is often befuddling. Just as the rest of our world has changed, so too are aging bodies. Without the ability to research the plethora of mysteries accompanying the body's changes, many elderly have no idea what is happening. Uncertainty can lead to confusion, embarrassment, isolation, and depression.

BRAIN CHANGES

Have you noticed your brain changing with age? Recall the days when you could remember the names of those you just met, and now you forget before they have finished introductions. We have all seen it in ourselves and observed it with the elderly. As much as we wish it away, neurological changes happen every day of our lives. Several things are taking place in the aging brain. It is common by the mid-60s to have decreased ability to remember things quickly, and it takes a longer time to do calculations. However, the elderly should be able to complete the calculations and retrieve the word they are trying to say in a short period of time.

Science has taught us that the brain gradually shrinks as we get older. However, memory changes are not directly related to decreasing brain mass. As the brain is shrinks, the balance center of the brain, called the cerebellum, becomes smaller too. This part of the brain relies on information from other body parts to maintain balance. The eyes, ears, and sensory input from the feet help the body remain stable. With the shrinking cerebellum, and the decreased input from other organs, many elderly feel very unstable as they stand. This is considered a normal consequence of aging and is expected as your parent reaches their 80's. If this happens earlier, it could be indicative of other issues. Inform the doctor if your parent experiences balance issues. Provide as much information as possible so that the problem can be addressed.

Memory loss is categorized into thee types. The first is the normal age-related decrease in brain function. The second type is called mild cognitive impairment. Mild impairment manifests primarily as short-term memory loss without the loss of independent function. The third type is dementia. Dementia is a word used to describe decreased brain function severe enough to inhibit the ability to live independently.

Alzheimer's disease is the most common type of dementia. But there are other types of dementia due to anatomic problems of the brain, like a brain tumor or too much fluid on the brain. Also, dementia can be related to brain inflammation or nutritional deficiencies such as low vitamin B12 and changes in electrolytes such as potassium or sodium. Other medical conditions such as thyroid problems can cause dementia. Stroke or mini-stroke can also cause dementia.

Since it is sometimes difficult to tell where the person falls in the memory loss spectrum, screening tests are performed by the doctor. Simple tests can be done in the primary care provider's office. According to Dr. Fagan, as a general rule, shorter tests help rule out significant memory loss. However, if there is serious memory loss, more intensive testing may be needed requiring a referral to a neurologist.

FEET

Feet are often overlooked by caregivers as well as those walking upon them. This is unfortunate because feet can be a great indication of how well a body is doing. With aging there is a gradual decrease in the strength of the ligaments holding the toes and bones of the feet together. This loss of strength can cause deformities of the feet, leading to bunions, hammertoes, and loss of the foot's arch. Sometimes the aging person may not realize that unsteady walking is due to issues with feet. It's essential to have the doctor look at your parents' feet. Seniors may develop dry skin on the bottom of their feet, and daily moisturizer is needed. Watch for deep cracks in the skin on the bottom of their feet. Bacteria can get in the cracks and cause an infection. If there are cracks around the heel, it can make it painful for the elderly parent to walk.

If your loved one has diabetes, you must pay particular attention to the cracks. Imagine any open crack as a conduit for bacteria to invade the body. Even a slight crack on the heal could allow bacteria to invade a weakened body.

Examine your loved one's toenails. Nails that change can indicate hypothyroidism, peripheral artery disease (PAD), or fungal infection of the toenails. As seniors age, the toenail becomes thicker and harder to trim. Having a podiatrist examine your parents' feet once a quarter is a good idea. As your parents age, clipping their own nails can be challenging. You need to ask them if you can check their feet and help trim the nails. You may want to take them for monthly pedicures in-between visits to the podiatrist.

HEARING

Like Sharon, you may have noticed your parents' straining to hear you. The reason we lose hearing with age is due to the tiny hair cells in the inner ear becoming damaged. These cells don't regrow. This type of hearing loss is called sensorineural hearing loss. Age related hearing loss occurs to some degree in almost half of all adults over 65. It is known as presbycusis. Exposure to loud noises over a life time may cause damage to hearing nerves or parts of the brain responsible for processing sound. Another type of hearing loss is called conductive hearing loss and is usually due to a blockage in the middle or outer ear. The most common blockage is caused by a buildup of wax. Sometimes there is a combination hearing loss, called mixed hearing loss due to both sensorineural and conductive influences. It is important for elderly to address hearing loss to minimize the impact on physical and cognitive abilities. Signs to watch for are difficulty understanding words, trouble hearing consonants, asking others to repeat, muffling of speech, need to have TV or Radio volume loud, withdrawal from conversations and avoidance of social interactions.

VISION

With age, the lenses of the eyes become less flexible causing them have trouble focusing on close objects, a condition called presbyopia. As your lens becomes less flexible it can no longer change shape to focus on close-up images. That's why nearly everyone needs reading glasses as they reach their mid-40s or 50s. Other age-related eye problems are cataracts, glaucoma, and macular degeneration.

Cataracts: Cataracts are a clouding of the normally clear lens of the eye.

Glaucoma: Glaucoma is a group of eye conditions that damage the optic nerve. It is usually related to high pressure in the eye and can cause blindness.

Macular degeneration: Macular degeneration is caused by a disorder retina.

There are two types of macular degeneration, wet and dry. Wet is a due to growth and leakage of blood beneath the retina while dry is the result of aging and the thinning of the macula (small central part of retina). There are some treatments for wet, but as of printing nothing has been approved for dry macular degeneration. Don't ignore any eye problems. The progression of wet macular degeneration can be slowed with early treatment.

IMMUNE SYSTEM

The immune system changes as we get older. As a general rule, the immune system gradually decreases with age, especially in local tissues that are needed to help fight infection. This can happen in an older woman's urethra (the duct from the bladder to the urinary meatus). It explains why our aging moms and grandmothers have more urinary tract infections (UTIs). UTIs can smolder for a long time before you or your parents notice something is off. You may see your parent one week and they are fine, but the following week, they are mentally off. Don't chalk it up to dementia because it may be a UTI. Encourage your parents to drink lots of fluids. Cranberry juice has been studied, and the evidence that it prevents a UTI is not substantiated. It won't hurt you, but there is no need to force it upon a person.

All of this information may cause you to question your own current anti-aging regimens. Is it possible to minimize the consequences of aging? The scientific answer is both yes and no. So far, evidence-based scientific research has not discovered the fountain of youth, but it has revealed lots of data to help us understand issues that increase risk in an aging body.

MEDICAL VISITS

When accompanying senior parents to a physician, parents might not want to discuss what they consider private, intimate matters in front of their children. Darla went with both of her parents to various doctor appointments. As she explained to friends, her mom was a piece of cake and would discuss virtually everything and anything with her doctor. Her dad, who usually was very chatty, clammed up at the doctor's office. He did not want Darla to know of his issues and would become angry when she asked him to explain. Unfortunately, this caused much stress on both sides of the relationship. He still saw her as his daughter, his baby girl, and because of that alone, he didn't want her to know his physical ailments. Darla was frustrated because she wanted to find solutions to help make his life easier, but her dad perceived it as an intrusion.

Dr. Fagan advised Darla to open up the communication and explain clearly her objectives for needing to know personal issues. When she told her dad why having certain information was necessary for his protection and health, he began to be more forthright. Was there still some head-knocking and total frustration on both sides? Yes, of course, but Darla's father began to see that she was trying to do what would benefit him most. Darla talked to both parents when everyone was calm and not rushing and frustrated. Although her dad was initially a little on the combative side, he began to soften and provide more information to her and the doctor.

CHAPTER 2

How do we avoid or minimize the consequences of aging?

FOUNTAIN OF YOUTH

PROPER DIET

Avoid high-fat foods and refined sugars. Sugar, in particular, creates changes that may damage cells and increase inflammation. If one of your parents is complaining about frequent urination and their joints hurting, notice their sugar intake.

Sarah, a patient of Dr. Fagan's, loved and enjoyed sweets her whole life. She did not have diabetes or weight issues, so her daughter Jill assumed it was fine. At one of the appointments, Sarah complained that her joints were hurting more than usual. Dr. Fagan asked Sarah about her sugar intake. Sarah sheepishly looked at Jill as she replied, "Oh, I eat them once in a while." Jill interjected, "Mom, do you pay attention to what you eat?" Jill exposed the truth by explaining that her mom enjoyed cookies or other desserts at lunch and dinner. She also had a couple of pieces of chocolate candy every afternoon. Add a donut or pastry at church and sugary breakfast cereal once or twice a week, and it's completely understandable why her joints were hurting. Sarah believed there was no concern as long as she was also eating a healthy diet with some vegetables. Dr. Fagan suggested Sarah cut back on sugar until her next visit, and they would compare how her joints felt then. One month later, Sarah admitted her joints were not as achy.

EXERCISE

Often the elderly are fully aware they **need** to exercise but haven't found the right kind of exercise that appeals to them. The earlier in life they start exercising, the more it helps to decrease the aging effect and dementia. But don't despair if they haven't started yet. Even people in their 80s and 90s can improve their balance and increase their muscle mass.

Exercises such as Tai Chi can help to establish balance and maintain the strength of your loved one's lower extremities. This can be very beneficial in helping to reduce the risk of falling. It will also reduce mental and physical stress. It can help minimize bone loss for women, aids in the reduction of arthritis pain, and lowers blood pressure. Tai Chi movements with mental imagery help to integrate the mind and body. It enhances your loved one's mental capacity and concentration and promotes faster recovery from heart attacks and strokes. Tai Chi has been shown to improve conditions such as Parkinson's, M.S., and Alzheimer's.

There are many videos online where your loved one can do the exercises in the comfort of their own home. Because Tai Chi is done slowly, your senior won't feel overwhelmed trying to keep up with others. Tai Chi can be done while seated, too, so don't let there be excuses.

Walking is considered the perfect form of exercise, because every major muscle group in the body is used. It can help to improve bone density and reduces the risk of osteoporosis. Walking every day has the added benefit of your loved one being outdoors, getting fresh air and sunshine, and can help keep the mind alert.

Balance exercises at any age are beneficial. Encourage your loved one to find several activities they would like to do. The elderly can do balance exercises while sitting or standing. Holding onto a chair or countertop is a great way to foster confidence while working on balance. Better balance helps to eliminate the risk of falling. It's another way to keep your parents in their home as long as and safe as possible.

Falls are the leading cause of injury to those 65 years and older. Seniors are likelier to break a bone or incur a head injury with a fall. Falls without damage take a mental toll. Even when seniors aren't injured, they may become so fearful of another fall they cut back on daily activities. If you notice this, encourage them to get out and walk daily. Perhaps you or a friend can walk with them. Remind them that a body in motion stays in motion. They need to try to have some movement daily.

AVOID ALCOHOL AND SMOKING

Alcohol consumption for the aging parent may be an issue. People who previously drank very little may suddenly develop a desire for alcohol. Increased consumption can lead to potentially dangerous falls and broken limbs. Alcohol and many medications do not go well together. When mixed with medicine, a new or heavier reliance upon alcohol can potentially cause an accidental overdose. If your loved one consumes too much, you may want to hide it or keep it out of the house. If their dependence on alcohol increases, you should discuss it with their doctor. It is recommended only one drink per day for women and no more than two for men.

Of course, smoking is known to increase the risk of multiple cancers, as well as lead to plaque buildup in the arteries. This makes the arteries less strong, and increasing the risk of memory loss.

WORK THAT BRAIN

About four years ago, Sharon started noticing her mom was starting to forget things. Important things like accidentally setting the kitchen on fire...three times. She seemed confused about how the frying pan with an inch of oil caught on fire. Sharon took her mother to a neurologist. He said she had the beginnings of cognitive impairment or dementia. Sadly, this was one of her mom's biggest fears. Longevity ran in the family where it was not uncommon for someone to live to be 95 to 98 years old. Her grandfather had lived to be 96 and had dementia for the last six years of his life. Sharon's mom was acutely aware of the tragedy of dementia, did not want it to happen to her, yet she could not recognize any signs of this memory loss in herself.

There may be a genetic tendency toward dementia, but this is also not inevitable. Generally, whatever is good for the heart is good for the brain. So proper diet, exercise, and avoidance of excessive alcohol and smoking can reduce the risk of dementia.

Treating the brain like a muscle that needs exercise is essential as we age. It is vital to engage in activities that require thinking. It's important to vary the activities. For example, if your senior loves crossword puzzles, adding a jigsaw puzzle is a good idea. If the brain only practices puzzles, it will atrophy in other areas. Therefore, include some math or other critical thinking tasks in the brain exercise.

With Sharon's mother, it was evident that she was not able to cook meals unsupervised. Sharon, the clever caregiver, decided to unplug the stove to keep her mother from cooking. For a while, her mom was satisfied using only the microwave. But as she aged, it became necessary to move her parents to an assisted living facility. Although her mom can't recall what she ate for breakfast, she can still play bridge and other card games, all while keeping an accurate score.

She enjoys her living with other seniors.

We know how important it is to keep our loved one's brains engaged. Check into your local senior centers for classes and activities. Bring the grandchildren to visit with an intentional game to play. Here are some additional suggestions: card games, board games, dominoes, Sodoku, arts and crafts, and even Chess.

You may want to encourage them to learn to play a musical instrument or learn sign language. Crazy as it may sound, some seniors have even learned to juggle. Regardless of what you think you know about your parents; you may discover something new they've always wanted to learn or do. Try to find something fun, entertaining, and engaging for them. Now is the time to encourage them to push themselves to new brain-enriching activities.

LAUGH

A good chuckle not only makes you feel better mentally, but has health benefits too. Laughter stimulates your organs by the extra oxygen uptake inhaled during a good guffaw. This increases the endorphins that are released by the brain which relieves stress. It stimulates circulation and relaxes muscles. Laughing has prolonged effects on your immune system. It increases positive thoughts which help to fight off stress hormones. Don't let this overwhelm you. Even if you consider yourself to be lacking humor, have courage.

A sense of humor can be learned. It takes effort and a "can do attitude" but it can be developed. Try finding some funny comics, cards, or stories and reach for them every-morning. Watch silly comedies and browse funny articles. Spend time with friends and share some laughs. This is critical to helping you and helping your aging parents. Find something to make you all enjoy a good laugh. It will make all feel better.

CHAPTER 3

Talking about aging with your loved one.

THE OTHER TALK

Sharon and her two sisters had started trying to talk with their parents about the aging process to discover what their wishes were. It was an exercise in frustration and futility. Their dad refused to acknowledge that he and their mom would ever need help and would not talk about mortality. He was adamant they would live in their own home and not "go to some old people's place." He was very argumentative about everything related to aging. It took Sharon over two years to get him and her mom to give her just the songs they wanted to be played at their funeral, much less any of the other details.

Keep in mind; this wasn't one time asking for the details. Oh, no, Sharon asked twice a month for two solid years. The other two sisters had tried as well. The consensus among them was Sharon had finally worn their parents down enough to get the information. What was Sharon's secret? She eventually threatened to have Prince's 'Purple Rain' played at the conservative Presbyterian church service. You can laugh all you want, but sometimes you have to think out of the box to get the information you need from your parents.

Dying is a universal experience. Almost everyone has a story about how easy or hard a death was among those they love. The difference between these experiences may be whether we have shared our wishes for how we want to spend our final days. Death tends to bring out both the best and the worst in people and families. There doesn't appear to be a middle ground. Preparing before a parent's death can go a long way in keeping fluctuating emotions under control.

What is the most important and costly conversation we aren't having with our parents? The answer is, "What are their final wishes?"

THE CONVERSATION

Consider this, as reluctant as our parent(s) may be to discuss their last wishes, 90% percent of people think it is essential to talk about end-of-life wishes with their loved ones. Unfortunately, only 27% have done so. Are you hesitant to discuss end-of-life questions with a parent? You're not alone if you say yes. According to the Conversation Project, one in five people said they'd avoided the subject because they didn't want to worry about upsetting their loved one. Ask yourself if you're one of those people. If so, we have suggestions on how to get started.

How do you eat an elephant? One bite at a time. How do you get the answer to these end-of-life questions? One question at a time. You don't have to barricade your parents in the house for three hours to get the necessary answers. You can ask one or two questions at a time, write down their answers, and put the paper somewhere you can find it quickly and easily. Don't rely upon your memory for the answers. When a beloved parent dies, the adult children must take care of many details. Emotions can range from the sublime to the ridiculous, and that's just your emotions, much less the feelings your siblings bring to the table.

Asking the right questions, and choosing your words carefully, can help ease these meaningful discussions with your parents. Which question would you rather answer: "Hey, Dad, which assisted living facility do you want to live in for your final days?" or "Hey, Dad, I know you and Mom want to live here forever, which I 100% support, but, just in case you can't, which place would you like better – XYZ or ABC?"

In parenting a child, we were taught to ask them simple questions with only two choices. In sales, it's called the assumptive close. Just like children, this technique can help you with your aging parents. Older people think they have to give you an answer because it's an either-or question. It is a simpler way to get answers. It's a great way to learn some things about their wishes.

Most people say they want to die at home; however, over 60% of people die in a hospital or an institution. When you think of your own death, don't you hope that one morning, when you are old but not yet infirm, you just don't wake up? We all wish for this ending.

Instead of dreading asking your parents about how they want to live the rest of their lives, mentally picture it as a gift of love wrapped in knowledge. Treat them with respect. Do not talk down to your parents. Regardless of their mental function, they will hear the tone of your voice. Remember these discussions can be among the richest, most loving, and most intimate conversations you may ever have with your family.

Sharon and Darla each discovered their parents found it depressing to discuss end-of-life choices. Once they started easing into conversations with their parents, they found it was more about how they phrased the questions. Some parents feel like they're being attacked with questions. Sharon's dad wanted to "cogitate on things" before answering anything. Although it frustrated her, she agreed with him, stating, "that's fine. I think you should do that. I'll connect with you on Wednesday or Thursday." She smiled sweetly, and her dad nodded his head in agreement. He felt in control, and Sharon was happier because she knew she would get some type of answer within a couple of days.

By having several in-depth conversations at the kitchen table, a very familiar and safe environment for your parents, you avoid having to make critical, last-minute decisions in the emergency room. Studies show there is less guilt and depression when the family is prepared for health issues and end-of-life events. Families also have an easier time processing their grief.

Kitchen table conversations are so much easier than conversations in the Intensive Care Unit at a hospital. The decisions you make in the comfort of home with your loved ones are based on what they value the most. This will decrease stress and fear.

Jeanine, a passionate patient advocate, has witnessed when life-saving treatments did not work for a parent. She has watched families financially ruined because of poor decisions made while a loved one was battling cancer. Jeanine has seen the anxiety experienced by families as they try to understand what hospice is and is not. A key goal for all families and elderly parents is to have hard conversations before significant lifestyle changes happen. But if parents are still here, it's not too late to start "The talk".

Sharon and Darla turned to Jeanine for help with the right questions to ask their parents. Jeanine recommended The Conversation Project (see resources). Pulitzer Prize-winning author Ellen Goodman co-founded this in 2010 after serving as her mother's caretaker for many years. Your Conversation Starter Kit is a downloadable guide to help give people a jumping-off point for this all-important talk. Although Sharon and Darla had already started asking questions and had explained their thought process to Jeanine, she recommended the following method to guide them more efficiently in discussing quality of life with their parents.

GET READY

It would be best if you thought about your conversation with your parents before diving in. Create a binder with some pages so you can write answers. These preliminary questions and answers will eventually make their way to the back of the binder because the responses from the aged will be at the forefront of the binder. As you prepare, ask yourself these questions:

1. What do I need to think about or do before I feel ready to have the conversation? Sharon and Darla agreed that while they had thought beforehand about the questions, they wanted to ask their parents, they had not really thought about what they personally needed to feel in order to be ready to have the conversations with their parents. Their self-care was important. They started practicing self-care before meeting with their parents. They started asking

themselves how they felt physically, mentally, emotionally, and spiritually. If they were not in a harmonious state, they each decided they shouldn't ask life-care questions that day. They waited until they were prepared. You may want to start journaling your emotions. It can be beneficial to write down what you're feeling before asking your parents questions and then write down your feelings afterward. Why? You can easily see if your fears are getting in the way of what your loved one is trying to tell you. Seeing your fears clearly on paper can help you realize your fears may not be your parents' fears. This can open up a whole new door to understanding your parents.

2. What particular concerns do I want to bring up?
3. For many families, finances are a vital topic. Are your parents' finances in order?
4. Does a particular family member have power of attorney?
5. Do your parents have life insurance?
6. Have they prepaid their funeral arrangements?
7. Do they have a will?

The list goes on. Discuss the questions with siblings first to insure you are all coming to your parents with the same base of knowledge.

GET SET

You may think you know what your loved one wishes, but you may be surprised. Gentle prompting on your part will reveal what your parent wants. An example may be a soft question such as "What really matters to you at the end of your life?"

Sharon's dad responded with he wanted his family to know he loved them. Darla's dad wanted his wife of fifty years to know that she would be well cared for if he died before she did. Surprisingly, Sharon and Darla's mothers wanted to ensure that no one had to disrupt their lives to care for them. Understandably, none of us want to be a burden on others. But in reality, we will someday need help.

Share the "what matters to me" statement with the doctor. It also lets your parent know the family is following their wishes. It can prevent sibling differences. As you get answers to questions, add them to the binder. Allow your siblings to see what is important to your parents.

Tab this section as "Mom's wishes" and tab "Dad's wishes ". The template for your binder will be in the resources section.

Asking specific care questions helps to eliminate confusion, guilt, and remorse for both the parent and the caregiver. As you discuss the following questions with your parents, remember that this is about how they want to live. It may be very different than what you personally want or what you had previously thought they would desire. As you ask questions be sure to write the answers down and place them in the care binder.

1. What do you want the last phase of your journey in life to be like?
2. As a patient, how much do you want to know about your condition? Just the basics? All the details or something in between?
3. How much information should the doctors share with our loved ones?
4. Which family member will be the primary decision maker or has the power of attorney?
5. If you have been diagnosed with a terminal illness, do you want know how quickly it progresses?
6. Do you want to get treatment indefinitely, regardless of the discomfort and side effects, or do you want to have the option to focus on your quality of life over the quantity?
7. Do you want to spend your final days at home if possible or do you care if you are in a hospital or nursing facility?
8. When you are at the end of your earthly journey do you think you would rather be surrounded by love ones or in a more private setting?
9. Are there financial affairs you would like to get in order?
10. Are there family tensions that you want to resolve?

11. Who do you want (or not want) to be involved in your care and making decisions on your behalf?
12. Do you prefer to be actively involved in your healthcare decisions or have your doctors do what they think is best?
13. Are there treatments you want, or more specifically, do not want? For example, a feeding tube or resuscitation if your heart stops

This list is just a starting point; there are probably additional family issues and topics you need to discuss with your parents. Your healthcare team may have other additional questions.

GO!

Sharon and Darla were very emotionally drained from asking these questions. These talks may take an emotional toll on the caregivers, but persevere. You can plan to take a few days or weeks to get answers.

Darla shared that she was exhausted after spending time with her parents. "It was tough. I suddenly realized the light at the end of the tunnel was going to be dark. They're not coming back once they've gone. They're not on vacation." Preparation will help you recover and process thoughts after having tough talks.

The Conversation Project suggests an easy way to begin conversations about end-of-life care with the following statements.

1. "Mom/Dad, I need your help with something."
2. "I need to think about the future. Will you help me?"
3. "I was thinking about what happened to _____, and it made me realize..."
4. "Even though I'm okay right now, I'm worried that _____, and I want to be prepared."
5. "Remember how ____ died? Was that a 'good' death or a 'hard death'? How will yours be different?"

You can even ask friends, doctors, other caregivers, clergy members, or others to be involved in this process. You don't have to fly solo.

When is a good time to talk? Do you want to broach these questions at a family gathering, perhaps around the holidays? Keep in mind holidays are often a very stressful time for families. Consider discussing the questions around significant happy life events such as the birth of a child or grandchild or a child leaving for college.

Where would your loved one feel the most comfortable talking? At home, around a kitchen table? At a favorite restaurant or park? Perhaps a walk or a hike or at your place of worship?

Choose a setting where your parents will be the most relaxed and comfortable. Have them tell you the three most important things they want their family, friends, or doctors to know about their end-of-life wishes. Incorporate those wishes into the discussion. When parents hear their wishes said back to them, they tend to relax more, leading to deep and meaningful conversations.

Sharon recalls one of her first conversations with her dad about his wishes for the end of his life. The man stated there would "be plenty of time to think about that later." This Scarlett O'Hara concept of "I'll think of it all tomorrow, I can stand it then" is not a new one with the elderly. At the time of her dad's comment, he was in his mid-seventies and had already outlived everyone in his family by several years.

What do you want the last phase of your life to be like? This is the root question that needs to be answered. Keep that in the back of your inquisitive mind as you begin the conversation. As we mentioned, you don't have to do everything in one day. In most cases, it will be counterproductive and may result in hurt feelings or a complete refusal to discuss anything.

Keep in mind nothing is set in stone. You and your parents can revisit issues as circumstances change. If there are disagreements, try not to judge or become overly emotional. If you become irritated or riled up with one of your parents, take a break and, if necessary, reschedule your meeting for another day.

Asking the essential questions is the time for love and kindness, not accusations and bitterness. Tensions can build quickly. This is about helping your loved ones and not about who's right, so stay focused on your goals.

KEEP GOING

Woohoo! Congratulations! Pat yourself on the back. You've broken through the barrier. The initial conversation is the hardest. It's much easier to do the next one and the one after that and the one after that.

There are a few things that are important as you continue your caregiving journey. First, you must remember that although your parents are elderly, they are still your parents. They don't want you to boss them around. Heck, nobody likes being bossed. Remember to ask and not to tell them what to do. Use the respect and courtesy you would in conversation with your best friends. Your parents are aware that the generations are going at different speeds. They see the caregivers juggling a million things and moving at warp speed but they still need you to slow down and be patient when dealing with them. Although they might not know how to google or talk to Alexa, they are not stupid. They have years of wisdom behind them and they need some validation for their contributions and acknowledgment of their knowledge.

Helping our aging parents has an unknown yet inevitable end date. Knowing you will lose them can create anxiety for caregiving adults. It isn't easy to process these emotions. Give yourself time to go through the feelings and be gentle with yourself. Remember, it's just as hard on your parents as on you. Many of the elderly are more afraid about how they will live the end of their life versus the actual dying part.

1. What do you want your parents to remember about these conversations with you?
2. Is there anything you want or need to clarify?
3. Was there something you think was perhaps misinterpreted or misunderstood?
4. What do you want to talk about the next time?
5. Does a specific person need to be there?
6. Who is handling all of the paperwork?
7. Who has the power of attorney document?
8. Who is the healthcare surrogate? Does everyone in the family know who it is?

9. Do your parents have a living will?
10. Are these documents current, up-to-date, and accessible?
11. How are their bills being paid?
12. Is there income that can be re-directed for health care and caregivers if need be? If not, try to investigate Medicaid.
13. Is a child or relative on their checking account who can access funds if needed? It is advised to have 3 months of necessary funds in this account to help parents should they become unable to assume their usual financial obligations.
14. If you need to hire a caregiver other than a family member, how will they be paid? If children are assisting with expenses will they be repaid out of estate after the passing of parents?

All these questions must have written answers. Even though you and your siblings may be there and in agreement, things will inevitably come up, and each of you will have a different recollection. This is typical, and it's why you need to have it written down and shared with other family members.

Advance Directive

Now is the time to discuss an advance directive. You may have heard of it before but not know what it means. An advance directive is an umbrella term for defining and expressing how one wants to live and be treated. The state-approved advance directive documents will allow you to specify your wishes and appoint an individual to speak for you when you cannot do so yourself. Be sure to check with your state for more specifics. Each state has different requirements.

Other terms often used with advance directives: are living will, healthcare proxy, healthcare agent, DNR (Do Not Resuscitate), and POLST (Physician Order for Life-Sustaining Treatment).

The purpose of any advance directive is to enable your parents to speak for themselves and to let other people know what choices they have made and what is important to them. Until your parents create an advance directive, they are at the mercy of whoever is taking care of them. With an advance directive, any questions that arise will have an answer written in the document. A physician must sign POLSTs and

DNRs. Advance directives legally must contain certain
must be documented according to state rules. You de
attorney to complete an advance Directive and if it cont
state's provisions it becomes legally valid as soon as it is si̱
of witnesses. Be sure to comply with your state's law.

When are Advance Directives Implemented?

The only documents that dictate how first responders handle a
medical crisis are Do Not Resuscitate (DNR) or Physician Order for
Life-Sustaining Treatment (POLST). These written and signed documents clearly state what the patient wants or does not want the emergency medical responders to do at an accident site, or home if the
patient is not breathing and or the heart has stopped. Cardio
Pulmonary Resuscitation (CPR) often cracks the fragile ribs of the
elderly and may leave them alive but with brain damage. Is this something they are willing to endure at their age? Emergency personnel must
try, at all costs, to bring them back to life unless there is a visible DNR
or POLST. If your aging parents DO NOT want to attempt aggressive
measures, have them keep their desires visible. Emergency responders
can only honor POLST and DNR orders. Other advance directives,
POA, living will, healthcare proxy, etc., are not acceptable by EMTs. If
911 has been called and you do not have a POLST or DNR to show
EMTs, they will have to do what is needed to stabilize and transfer the
patient to the hospital. The advance directives can be implemented after
the patient has been transferred to a hospital and the physician has eval-
uated the patient.

Advance directives do not expire. An advance directive remains in
effect until your parents change it. If they complete a new advance directive, it invalidates the previous one. As families and circumstances
change, you and your parents should review the advance directives to
ensure they still reflect your parents' wishes. If they have a change in
what they desire at the end, a completely new document must be
drawn up.

Five Wishes

Five Wishes is an easy-to-use legal advance directive document
written in everyday language. It helps adults at any age or health to

consider and document how they want to be cared for at the end of life. It is America's most popular living will, with more than 40 million copies in circulation.

What are your five wishes?

1. The person I want to make healthcare decisions for me when I can't
2. The kind of medical treatment I want or don't want
3. How comfortable do I want to be
4. How I want people to treat me
5. What I want my loved ones to know

It's better to have a plan before your parent becomes incapacitated. Many parents are relieved to have an adult child willing to step up and help them plan.

Advance directives may change as you age.

The most helpful advance directive varies by where you are in life. When you are young and healthy, it's about speaking in general terms about your priorities. When a person develops a chronic condition or illness, they have a clearer idea of what may happen and can be more specific about what they want. When a person has a life-limiting condition, it becomes essential to be explicit about their wishes

Guidelines at various stages:

- **You are healthy.** You want to complete an advance directive so if something suddenly happens and you can't speak for yourself, others will know what you want in general terms. If nothing else, COVID has taught us that unexpected things happen.
- **You have a chronic condition.** Because you know about your disease and its course, you can be more specific in saying what you do and don't want.
- **You have a serious illness.** You can be more specific in saying what you do and don't want. Depending on the predicted course, you may also want to complete a POLST.

- **You know that you don't have long in this w**
  advance directive may be useful as it contains m(
  information and nuances than the POLST, but
  physician signed POLST to specify what life sav
  treatments you are willing to endure at the end of your life.

PRACTICAL APPLICATIONS TO APPLY AS SOON AS POSSIBLE

Power of Attorney (POA)

Power of attorney (POA) actually refers to two separate directives. One is for financial estate planning, also called durable power of attorney and the other is to manage health care decisions. Basic power of attorney templates may be available on line.

Enhanced power of attorney, such as one that will allow for gifting down of an estate to qualify for Medicaid require a visit to an estate attorney. Be sure to have the advance directive drawn up and added to the binder. If your parents know what life saving measures they want or don't want, have a physician signed POLST posted.

Hopefully, your parents will already have a Last Will and Testament. We encourage you to have one drawn up as soon as possible if they haven't. This document clearly spells out what your loved ones want to have happen with their personal belongings. This can even be done online in some states as long as it is notarized.

Take your parents to the bank and have your name added to their checking and savings accounts. Some families may open an additional joint account with a child's name on it simply to help pay parents' monthly bills. This can be easier for aging seniors to accept than you the adult child requesting to be on the same account. Upon the passing of your parent, this joint account can be easily closed.

Locate your parents' insurance policies and have the numbers written in the binder. Often overlooked, make sure you know where all deeds, and titles for all real estate, all vehicles, campers, etc., are located. You may want to spend an afternoon with your parents to insure you have all documents in a specific place or in the care binder. It is best to prepare before you are in need of these important documents.

Have your parents talk to all your siblings so everyone understands and knows what their wishes are. Now is the time for your parents to explain why their decisions were made and avoid lingering questions or hurt feelings. If this is written in the binder, your siblings can see what your parents said.

CHAPTER 4

Assess the Situation and Take Action.

AGING IN PLACE

There's no place like home. Home is where your parents want to live as long as possible. They've spent years there; it is where they feel the most comfortable and the safest.

Unfortunately, one out of three of those homes does not meet the changing needs of seniors. Family caregivers often worry about risks or fires in the home, perhaps the isolation of an elderly parent, and the overall safety in general of their loved one.

The Sandwich Generation, young to middle-aged adults raising their children and caretaking or supporting their aging parents, are busy. They often have jobs outside the home. Many juggle family responsibilities of parenting their children and even grand-parenting. Senior caregivers can have health concerns, financial burdens, and sibling disconnectedness. In many cases, the role of the parents' caregiver falls upon one child.

Adding to the stress of busy lives, the Sandwich Generation now faces home safety concerns for their parents. While 89% of older adults want to stay in their own homes as long as possible, approximately thirty percent of those homes are unsafe and don't meet the primary aging-in-place needs.

Parents become so used to and complacent in their own homes that they don't think about their safety as they age. There are many things you can do to accommodate the aging body. Both your own and your parents' home may need some adjusting. Assess the home and make changes.

BATHROOM

The bathroom is the number one place where accidents can happen so quickly. The bathtub, shower, toilet, and floor all have slippery surfaces where aging feet may slide out uncontrollably. Older folks' balance can be precarious at best. Many homes have two or three bathrooms, making it twice or three times the opportunity for a slip and fall. The bathroom is the most common place for a slip and fall accident in the home.

According to ABCNews.com, over 80% of bathroom injuries were caused by slips and falls. About 30% of those injuries were minor – small cuts, bruises, and scrapes; however, that means 70% of those injuries were more serious. Older people and women are far more likely to be injured in a bathroom. Most trauma-related incidents occur on or around the toilet. How can you make the bathroom safer for your beloved parent? Here are ten ways to take preventative measures to help eliminate or avoid potential slips and falls in the bathroom.

1. Toss the throw rugs: Many seniors keep a throw rug or bathmat on the floor. Believe it or not, this is the most common source of falls in their home. If your parent insists they cannot live without a bathmat or throw a rug on the floor, try stabilizing them with double-sided or slip-resistant tape. Also, make sure you tape the corners.
2. Preventing Tub Fall: The tub is the trickiest part of the bathroom. It can be slippery when dry but incredibly slick when taking a bath or shower. Place some nonslip strips, mats, or tiles in the tub or shower enclosure. Be sure to secure the corners on the carpet or rug. Adhesive helps to provide extra grip for elderly parents who, as they age, tend to have increasingly unsteady gait and balance problems.

They may be on various medications affecting their heart rate and sense of balance, especially when sitting in the tub and trying to stand up quickly. Also, their medication may drastically slow their reaction time from what they think may be happening to what is genuinely happening, which could lead to an accident.

3. Keep The Tub and Shower Clean: Because seniors' eyesight is often poor, they may not see soap residue or mold in the shower or tub. Be sure to help them keep it clean. Spraying mold and mildew spray on problem spots daily can help prevent mold from building up. You may need to help clean the bathroom for them or hire a cleaning service.

4. Keep The Floor Dry:If your parent has a tub with shower curtains, use a weighted shower curtain with a liner. This addition helps to ensure the water stays in the tub and does not spray all over the floor. Your parents may ask you to help them in and out of the shower/tub. Be sure to dry the floor entirely once they have finished their shower or bath.

5. Install Grab Bars or Rails: Balance becomes more precarious as we age. It's notably more dangerous in the bathroom, where seniors must lift themselves, and the floor is wet or slippery. Grab bars or rails installed in and around the bathtub, shower, and toilet provide added assistance in helping the senior to navigate the bathroom safely. Some elderly parents believe a towel bar is strong enough to hold them up. Not true! The towel bar can be pulled out from the wall and cannot hold the weight of someone pulling on it. Be sure to assess the bathroom situation yourself.

6. Oh, Say, Can You See? How bright is your parents' bathroom, particularly at night? Do they have a nightlight or illuminated light switch in the bathroom? Do they have a nightlight in the hallway? Install night lights with a yellow glow. The golden light is gentler on sleep rhythms. It will help them see without causing the serotonin surge that makes it harder to get back to sleep.

7. Raise the Toilet: As we age, it becomes much more of a challenge to stand up from a toilet seat that is too low. It takes much more effort to stand up from a low toilet seat, particularly for older women. Consider getting your loved ones a toilet seat extender or a toilet with a high base, particularly if they already have mobility issues.

8. Get A Bath or Shower Seat: Moving around or standing for long periods becomes challenging as we get older. One way to help ensure safety in the tub or shower is to get a bath or shower seat. Providing a place to sit makes it much easier to shower.

9. Install A Handheld Shower Head: With a handheld shower head, your parents can easily shower themselves safely when they are sitting on the bath/shower seat. Sitting helps to eliminate falls, and they are less likely to slip in the tub or shower.

10. Slow Down, You're Moving Too Fast: Encourage your mom or dad to slow down and enjoy their shower or bath. The last thing you want them to do in the shower or bath is to rush. Water is everywhere, and being in a rush almost guarantees a slip and fall.

STAY HOME

Sharon made an appointment for a Certified Aging in Place Specialist (CAPS), Ms. Wallace, to inspect her parents' bathrooms and suggest how they could be safer. She hoped her parents would listen to a licensed professional on the needed safety issues.

What did Ms. Wallace recommend? A grab bar on the bathtub wall, a walk-in bathtub where her mother could sit safely in the tub, or a seat in the shower. Ms. Wallace also suggested new faucet handles so her mother, with her arthritic hands, could comfortably turn the handles. A handheld shower-head would make showering easier. If they install a walk-in tub, Ms. Wallace suggested a bathmat adhered to the floor to prevent a slip upon leaving the tub.

For her dad's bathroom, she suggested an anti-slip floor and seat in the shower, a grab bar next to his toilet, and a bathmat secured to the floor.

Sometimes parents will come up with their own safety measures method because they are unwilling or unable to pay for the needed items. Suction grab bars are incredibly unsafe and will pull away from the wall without much pressure. Plastic lawn chairs in the shower or tub are NEVER a good idea. What do you do in situations like these? Explain to your parents how concerned you are about their safety. Remind them they want to stay in their own home as long as possible; professionally installed additions will help them.

As Ms. Wallace pointed out, bathroom grab bars are some of the best investments you can make for your parents in their home. Sometimes parents simply don't have the extra money to make the necessary changes in their bathrooms. Get a price for a professional to install grab bars and talk with your siblings about chipping in and paying for it. If one of your parents has served in the military, the VA (Veterans Administration) may be able to provide shower/tub seats, grab bar installation, and home cleaning.

As lovely as they are, walk-in tubs are relatively expensive, and your parents' water consumption will increase. The costs of these tubs may be prohibitive for the family.

HOME CLEANING

Let's address home cleaning. Vacuuming can become very difficult for the elderly. They often do not have the strength to push the vacuum around. Many people just decide not to vacuum or even dust. They no longer have the desire to maintain a clean home. It is no longer a high priority for them. Sometimes the change in the home happens quickly and can be a shock to visiting adult children.

On more than one occasion, Dr. Fagan has heard how adult children have been surprised to find their parents' homes in a state of messiness. "My mother was always such a fastidious homemaker," wailed one daughter. "Now their house looks like trailer trash."

Dr. Fagan explained, "Your mother is dealing with her mortality and strength and may not even know how to ask you for help."

Often seniors don't see what accumulates on the walls or corners. They overlook areas that need cleaning and often don't have the energy to keep up with the house or yard.

Rather than trying to make them feel badly about how their home looks, offer to help clean it up, or you can hire a cleaning service to help once every couple of weeks.

FINANCIAL CREATIVENESS

No one-size solution fits all families. It can be very stressful to watch your parents and feel helpless. If your parents are on a tight budget, you may consider creating a slush fund that will be funded by all the adult children, not just the adult child with the role of caregiver. Having some money stored for the aging needs will help the family have the ability to hire additional help for parents as their needs increase. With time they will need more accommodations. You may also want to consult an Estate Attorney to see if your parents may be eligible for Medicaid. Medicaid may have resources to help with caregiving and will pay if long term nursing home placement is needed. Each state has different requirements on the amount of assets that individuals or couples may own to qualify for state funded Medicaid. There are state guided ways to decrease assets to allow them to qualify. Consult an attorney for guidelines in your state.

Other sources of funding could come from the Veterans Administration, or can be found on the AARP website or at Aging.gov. We have listed resources at the end of the book, but check your city, state, and local organizations.

BRIGHTEN THEIR SURROUNDINGS

Your parents may be struggling with their mortality, depressed about their physical limitations, upset or frustrated about their lack of financial resources, friends dying, things they thought they would accomplish in their lifetime but haven't, or any of these things. This sadness may be a factor that some simple changes can help alleviate.

Chances that your parents have not had the interior of their home painted in many years. Soft colors play an essential part in the overall mental health of seniors. A newly painted living room, bathroom, and bedroom can brighten their mental outlook considerably. Sharon and Darla decided to combine their efforts and would paint each other's parents' homes. They could get it done quickly, much less expensively than a handyman, and their parents wouldn't have to worry about having strangers in their home.

Pick one standard color scheme to flow throughout the house. It will make the space seem bigger. Add one or two accent colors for smaller areas. Accent colors create visual interest in the room but won't overwhelm the eye. You may also consider variations of the same color in lighter and darker shades to subtly generate more interest.

You can brighten a room with artwork, bedding, pillows, and accessories. Add a pop of color with a vase, colorful pillows, or coordinating throws in the same color scheme. Here's a hint: all these items can be easily put away or swapped out with alternative colors depending on the season. Changing the decorations with the seasons can give the rooms a fresh new look on a budget.

As seniors age, their eyes harden and can become yellow. As one senior confirmed to AARP, "It's as if you're looking at everything through amber-colored sunglasses." Because seniors' vision yellows with age, it becomes more difficult for them to distinguish the difference between greens and blues. Have you noticed if your parents have a problem with glare in their home? Perhaps the sunlight blasts through specific windows and creates a glare in the living room when they're trying to read or watch TV. Small changes, such as painting a room or adding colorful pillows, can bring a new sense of energy to your parents' home. It may also energize them to where they are getting more done around the house or in their personal life. It also helps to eliminate depression.

You can get some color ideas by visiting nearby senior living communities, where you'll notice distinguishing colors between rooms, especially between the bathroom and the bedroom. Painting contrasting colors at your parent's home can help the elderly know where they are, especially when they get up at night. The contrasting color will help to eliminate confusion for a half-awake parent. For example, if the bedroom is white, the bathroom could be ocean blue. You want something easy for them to differentiate so they know where they are if they awaken at night.

You may want to incorporate some of the same color schemes used in senior living communities. Here are a few of the most popular colors and their emotional benefits:

1. Green – Earthy and forestry greens promote healing, relaxation, and serenity
2. Blue – Shades of water and beachy blues help make people feel more at peace. It's a calming color and tends to reduce stress.
3. White – Light and bright shades of cream and white promote hope, spirituality, cleansing, and calming.
4. Yellow – Often associated with happiness and is seen as a cheerful color.
5. Red – Is known to be a stimulating color that signifies strength and alertness.
6. Brown – Earthy tones and espresso shades of brown stimulate balance.

STAYING IN TOUCH

What happens when adult children live out of state or are hours away? Are you aware of the various aging-in-place organizations, groups, and resources? Are there friends of your parents who can check on them periodically? If you are the sole caretaker and live a distance, you might need to get a local coordinator, such as a Certified Aging Specialist. The organization that credentials aging specialists, the Society of Certified Senior Advisors, has a list of Certified Senior Advisors in your parent's location. These educated and certified senior advisors charge fees to help you and your parents understand their journey. They can help you evaluate and hire caregivers, help you navigate the healthcare journey, and put the correct legal documents in place.

As a distance caregiver, getting in touch with your parents is essential. Things in the lives of seniors can change very rapidly. Talking to your parents helps to ease the loneliness they feel. If other siblings don't live nearby, ask them to have regular weekly calls. These talks will help your seniors feel cared for and loved. If you lack conversational tools, try asking them a question about their younger days. When your parents talk, it can open up avenues of dialogue and provide connections to relieve loneliness. Write down your conversations in a journal or add them to the binder. You are gifting all of you as you learn more about their memories and feelings. If you share this in the binder, you are blessing others too. With these conversations come a greater understanding of your parent. You will begin to see them more as a person than as a parent. This is stress-reducing for both of you. We promise you will not regret this new depth of your relationship.

We understand that caregiving for your parent or any other person is difficult. Adult children, particularly the Sandwich Generation, are so busy with their own lives and may view it as a burden, a chore, to check in with their parents. Old emotions tend to surge a little higher, tempers run slightly shorter, and resentment may kick in. Linda, in her mid-forties, admitted she felt angry that her parents were getting old and couldn't do as much as they used to. She still needs help juggling her family. She found herself resentful that her parents were now requiring more of her. Some days she was exhausted. Some days she felt her siblings should be doing more. She felt guilty about being angry, which robbed her of joy. Linda started on a downward spiral which was not helpful for anybody. She realized she needed to seek some mental help for herself and found a therapist to help her. Therapy helped her to become a better caregiver and allowed her to renew herself.

TO DRIVE OR NOT TO DRIVE

Remember how excited you were when you got your driver's license and could now legally drive anywhere? Driving represents freedom and independence to an aging parent. They are still in control of their lives. Age-related physical and mental changes will happen. These changes can make driving more of a challenge and dangerous for the elderly. Changes don't occur at a specific age. Bill worried about his dad driving and asked the Highway Patrol in his state for recommendations. Here are their suggestions.

Tips To Keep Your Parents Safe on the road

1. Seat belts: Some elderly parents seem to forget occasionally to use their seatbelts. Remind them to wear them. If they're having problems remembering to use their seatbelts, you may want to evaluate if your loved one should be driving. If their seatbelt is uncomfortable, purchase a shoulder pad to make it more comfortable.

2. Cell phone: Seniors typically don't use their cell phones when driving; however, if your parents do, suggest they turn it completely off or turn it to vibrate so they can look at it later when they're not driving.

3. Do not eat while driving:If your loved has to eat or have a snack for medical/health reasons, have them pull off the road and into a parking lot to eat.

4. No alcohol and driving: Alcohol slows reaction time down as we age. Seniors should not drive, whether daytime or nighttime when they consume alcohol.

5. Limit distractions :Seniors aware of aging find they must pay attention as they drive. They may find they can no longer listen to the radio or audiobooks as they drive.

6. Watch the road:Depth perception changes as we get older. Encourage your parents to stay at least half a car length from the car in front of them. Encourage them to use familiar roads and not take unnecessary risks.

7. Drive during daylight as much as possible:Older adults have more trouble with night vision than they do during the daytime. Darkness and glare make it harder to see at night, which causes the possibility of more accidents

8. Avoid driving in bad weather:Rain and fog make it hard for all drivers. Snow is hazardous. Let your parent know they should not be driving during bad weather.

9. Choose a safer route:Left-turn mishaps increase as reactions decrease with age. Encourage your parent to make right-

hand turns only. Tell them to drive like FedEx and UPS and only make those right-hand turns even if they need to go out of their way a little bit. Highways, busy roads, and short on-ramps can be challenging to merge into oncoming traffic. Encourage your loved one to stick to familiar routes.

10. Avoid busy times on the road: Rush hour traffic can be a headache for anyone. It's particularly challenging for seniors. They may not know how close they are to the cars in front and behind them. Please encourage them to drive during non-rush hour times.

11. Don't drive when traffic is heavy: If your town or city has a university or professional football team, let your loved one know they should not drive during heavy traffic, either several hours before or after the game.

12. Are you stressed or tired: Be rested and calm when driving, or don't go. Many factors add to the dangers of driving, so if a senior is tired or worried about something, ask another person to drive or use Uber or a taxi. There have been many situations where a senior is frantically following medical transport of the spouse to the hospital and ends up in a traffic accident.

13. Know your medications: if your parents are taking medications that make them sleepy, they should not drive.

Don't forget, the right to drive is a privilege granted by the state where you live. Older people view driving as their last bit of independence. Most families don't want to be the bad guys in telling the parent to not drive. Families frequently ask Dr. Fagan to tell their parent they should not drive. In some situations, it will be obvious for Dr. Fagan to give his opinion. However, it is not easy for you or the doctor to decide. You must weigh their independence verses safety. If it is obvious to everyone (someone with repeated accidents or getting lost), and the parent still demands on driving, then the doctor can contact the DMV to recommend that the patient come in for driving evaluation.

TELEPHONE

Landlines are not as ordinary as they used to be; however, many older adults still have them. If your parents use a landline, make sure they have caller ID. Caller ID will allow a way to periodically check on who may be phoning your parents. If you find phone numbers on their current list that you don't recognize, particularly out-of-state or 800 numbers, and they're more than a couple of minutes long, you should ask your parents who it was and what that caller wanted. Sadly, our elderly are prey to phone scammers. Scammers will listen and pretend to care about your parent to gain trust. We know many elderlies enjoy chatting with others and scammers use this as a way to groom their prey.

Sharon's dad was particularly prone to talking to unknown people on the phone. He thought it was rude to hang up on them. Sharon tried to tell him he was being set up to be scammed. He didn't believe her until he had a charge of $346.29 on his credit card bill. He was sure Sharon had used his card for something and hadn't told him about it. Not true. This situation took a long time to be sorted out.

INTERNET

Parents may be elderly, but most are at least somewhat savvy about internet use. Many sites on the internet require passwords.

Do you have a list of these passwords? If they are hesitant to provide them to you, explain that if something unexpected happens, you may need to gain access to their computer. You may need to pay some bills or do their banking. What about various security questions? Do you know what those might be? Too often, spouses believe the other spouse has all the information, but in reality, and under stress, the spouse may forget. Many spouses don't know each other's passwords or where items are stored on the computer, and often, they can't recall their spouse's Social Security number.

FINANCIAL ACCOUNTS

It's time to have a conversation about financial accou
givers have no idea where their parents bank, hold inv
credit cards, or who the mortgage company may be. D
they have a financial advisor? If they have stocks, have tney authorized
anybody to make decisions about the stocks if they cannot do so? Do
you know what they want to have done with those stocks upon a
catastrophic illness or death?

You don't need to know the balances on accounts unless they are
comfortable with sharing, but you should know where they bank and
how to access investments. You are advised to write down their PINs
and bank account numbers. You can keep this information secure in
your own home, so they need not worry that it will be stolen from their
house.

Have them show you where they keep their legal documents. You
should know where they keep their power of attorney, will, trust, real
estate, tax, and insurance forms. Write down contacts for attorneys,
broker-dealers, accountants, and insurance agents. You need to have the
contacts written down so that if they cannot make decisions, you can do
it for them.

Financial responsibilities is often more complicated with if is a
blended family. In this case it is important to be certain that the child
who is assisting the elderly is honest and has no personal motive. Attorneys are familiar with family situations and are a good place to start
when your parents begin to investigate financial resources.

Does your mother have a "he account?" That's an account "he
doesn't know about." Many spouses will have an additional bank
account that the other may not know about. If so, is there an additional
signer on this account?

Do you know how much income they receive monthly and from
which sources?

Do you know what the bills are and which account they are paid
from.

Do they have automatic payments for their electric, telephone, utilies, rent/mortgage, and credit cards? Which one of your parents typically handles the money and bill paying?

Talking with family regularly about current scams and how to recognize them is also a best practice.

CREDIT CARDS

Oh, boy, where do we start on this? Opposites attract, and so goes the old saying. One parent may be an economic dynamo when handling money, and the other may be a spendthrift.

One parent may hide the credit card bills from their spouse, and the other may pay off the credit card statements as soon as they arrive.

You should know what credit cards each parent has, what the balance is, what the interest rate is, and when it is due. You may want to create a form; there are a lot of free forms online (see resources) with that information.

Here's a tip most people don't do, but it is incredibly helpful. Take all of your parents' credit cards and photocopy them. This way if there is ever any question about credit cards, or if they get misplaced, or stolen you will easily know who to notify. Also, have your parents pay for services and goods with a credit card versus a debit card. It is much easier to dispute a credit card charge and get a refund than a debit card. With a debit card, receiving a refund on fraudulent charges can be almost impossible.

PAYING MEDICAL BILLS

1. Often times the paying of medical bills becomes a challenge. Seniors usually have many specialists and sometimes hospital visits that all come with a price. The bills are confusing and may become overwhelming for the elderly. We suggest breaking it down in to a few steps.
2. Review the bill for accuracies. Compare to the Insurance company Explanation of Benefits (EOB). Verify all charges, especially hospital charges.
3. Make sure the insurance company has paid their portion.

4. Verify the charges.
5. If you spot errors, notify the provider and the insurer. Write down names of those you have spoken to and the date.
6. If your loved one is uninsured, ask the provider for a discount.
7. If they are unable to pay in full, ask for a zero-interest payment plan.
8. Don't ignore the bill. Providers are sending patients to collections much quicker these days.

If you or your parents are too overwhelmed to properly investigate bills, you may want to hire a medical claims billing advocates or claims assistance professionals. They will help you review bills, verify charges are accurate, and help reduce costs. There are organizations to help, such as CoPatients.com, Billadvocates.com, and Claims.org

DECLINING MENTAL FUNCTION AND THE CHAOS IT CAN CAUSE

One spouse may recognize that the other partner is changing and attribute it to old age. The spouse may never think to tell an adult child about changes because these changes can be so subtle. No one is paying close attention.

Or, even if the person notices things changing and discusses it with the doctor, that discussion is not shared with the other family members. Parents may also forget or refuse to take medication prescribed for the condition.

Even the caretaker may not recognize signs of early dementia or Alzheimer's; however, once they do, they should seek medical assistance to determine the best course of action and treatment for the patient.

IT'S ABOUT YOU TOO

As you can see, many dynamics are involved with aging parents. It's not just about them. It's also about you. More importantly, because you are now the one becoming a caregiver to your parents, you are having to mentally shift and make new adjustments in your life and your emotions. What can you do to make it easier for all concerned? Saying you're going to move to Costa Rica isn't the answer, although that might be fun. Remember the famous Girl Scout motto? "Always be prepared." As you read on, you are preparing like a good scout!

Your Chance to Help Someone Else

"In the heart of every caregiver is a knowing that we are all connected. As I do for you, I do for me." — *Tia Walker*

Let's take a breather for a moment. Think about how you were feeling when you first sought out this book. The chances are, you were anxious, overwhelmed and pursuing all avenues in the hope of finding answers

Hearing the distress in Sharon's voice as she told us about her parents was the catalyst for us writing this book. We knew she wasn't the only one struggling, and we realized how crucial it is for there to be easy to find information and guidance as we navigate the aging journey.

Our goal was to gather all the most pertinent information into one resource... and now we'd like to ask for your help in enabling more people to access it.

By leaving a review of this book on Amazon, you'll show other readers where they can find the help they're looking for.

Simply by letting other people know how this book has helped you and what they'll find inside, you'll highlight a road to reliable and accessible information that will make their journey that little bit easier.

Thank you for your support. This is something most of us have to deal with at some point in our lives; when we share information, we can make it a little easier on us all.

PLEASE REVIEW HERE

Click on hyperlink or scan QR code to be taken to review

CHAPTER 5

Choices and decisions.

PRIORITIZE

L iving arrangements, medication, health insurance, and financial issues are priorities. There may be options you haven't considered or even know about for your parents. We will explore a wide variety of topics that can assist you and your family tremendously in making these tough decisions and choices.

IN-HOME CARE

Keeping your parents in their own home as long as possible does not necessarily mean all the care must fall on one family member. Ideally, in a perfect world, several willing caregivers with unlimited time and treasure unite as a team to provide care for mom and dad. Unfortunately, this is not where many families find themselves. But that does not mean you must go at it alone.

If you can't find free services mentioned previously, consider hiring in-home care. There are small independent care agencies and larger corporate-run groups. After talking with neighbors, your parent's physician, or others that may have required help, consider googling options in your community. Compare rates and yelp reviews.

Are you aware of the myriad tasks and services in-home care companies offer?

They may include the following assistance for your loved one:

1. Assisting with appearance by bathing and grooming
2. Help them move about
3. Help the bedridden get in and out of bed
4. Assist with toileting needs and help the incontinence
5. Prepare and serve meals, and help feed those needing assistance
6. Care for the cognitively impaired
7. Medication administration or reminders
8. Take elders on outings to shop or other fun activates
9. Support for exercise programs
10. Help keep an eye on physical and emotional changes
11. Help identify fall risks and help you implement fall prevention
12. Provide companionship for your parents
13. Share activities that bring a smile and provide mental stimulation
14. Laundry and housekeeping
15. Errands and grocery shopping
16. Drive your loved one to and from medical appointments
17. 24-hour care if needed
18. Respite Care For Family And Loved Ones
19. Short-term relief for primary caregiver responsibilities
20. Referrals to medical professionals, support groups, and resources

Other Senior Care Services May Include

- 24-hour care (around the clock)
- Alzheimer's and dementia specialized programs

FINDING THE RIGHT IN-HOME CARE PROVIDER

There are many reputable in-home care providers across the U.S. It can be challenging to weigh the right choices for you and your family.

Which agencies are best for your parents? For some agencies, caring is a job. For other agencies, it can be a calling.

How do you make the best decision? Here are a few questions to ask:

1. How do you help with care to help seniors emotionally?
2. How long has your company been in business?
3. What do you do to keep the family involved in care?
4. Do you have a certain way to find the best caregiver for my parent?
5. Does your agency have liability coverage?
6. Are caregivers bonded and insured for theft?
7. Are employees required to have background and driving checks?

Check with your state on requirements. Not all states require this.

1. Are all of the caregivers employees of your company (not contract workers), and does workers' compensation cover them?
2. Do you have a good way of knowing when your caregivers come and go in a client's home?
3. May I come and meet some of your staff?
4. Do you have 24/7 call coverage?

WHAT IS THE DIFFERENCE BETWEEN INDEPENDENT AND ASSISTED LIVING?

Independent living communities focus predominantly on serving the social needs of the residents. They can live independently without much support.

Assisted living communities are for those who need assistance with daily living activities while allowing them to live as independently as possible. Assisted living may also be called residential care.

. . .

Independent Living

Independent living is designed exclusively for seniors. They may include retirement communities, retirement homes, senior housing, and senior apartments.

It's perfect for older adults who want to live in an active community, free from daily chores such as house maintenance, cooking, or housekeeping.

In one sense, they are like mini-college campuses where people of similar ages live together in a community, providing socialization activities. The housing is more compact and easier to navigate than living in a large home.

Assisted Living

Once your parent can no longer live independently, the next step may be a residential care facility. The term residential care is a broad term that refers to non-medical custodial care. This care can be in an assisted living facility or small board and care (sometimes called a guest home, or six pack). Board and Cares (BNCs) are usually houses in residential neighborhoods. The majority of board and care homes are licensed for six residents but may go up to twenty.

Regulations for services for assisted living and board and care facilities are the same, however the actual services offered may vary greatly. Board and Cares' have the ability to apply for special additional licensing to allow them to provide greater in home care. For example, if your parent needs any intravenous treatments, it is most convenient to have them at a facility that can allow for in-home nursing care.

It pays to do due diligence and ask a lot of questions. You need to know your options when a parent considers moving into an ALF or BNC. Typical services include staff available 24 hours a day, meals, medication management, bathing, dressing, housekeeping, and sometimes transportation. Most ALFs and BNCs have group dining and common areas for social and recreational activities.

Visit as many ALFs and BNCs in your area as you can BEFORE it becomes critical for your parents to move into one. Take your parents with you to see what you like in each community.

63

Some hints to know when visiting a community:

1. Sometimes, rents are negotiable. Near month end some facilities are often willing to restructure the rent down IF you ask for it. They may tell you 'no.' Don't accept this as the final answer. Ask to speak to the marketing or executive director and see if they're willing to be flexible on the rent. Many ALFs are corporate-owned and may have restrictions placed on them by the higher-ups. Conversely, sometimes the corporations have quotas, thus motivating the directors to negotiate with you. Look at a few and be forthright with the ALF that you are also looking at other facilities. This may be enough for them to negotiate some fees or even reduce the rent for a few months. Ask them, "What can you do for me (or your parents)?" You may be pleasantly surprised at their response.

2. Inquire about point systems. Points are a way that some ALFs determine if your senior needs more care. It attempts to quantify needs and set prices according to the care needed. Find out what factors will determine a price increase.

3. If looking at a Board and Care, ask if they are licensed to allow in home nursing medical care such as port flush or catheter changes. Some are licensed for this level of care. Most ALF's are not licensed, but you should ask anyway.

4. Some facilities charge to for simple added tasks such as putting on your parents' shoes; some include such care as routine. Be certain to get a list of what items are covered in the contract and what are the additional fees.

5. Ask how often your parents will receive showers. Does this include someone standing in the bathroom assisting your parent if necessary? Will the CNA help in dressing them? How often will their hair be washed? Will the CNA help dry it? Do they have a hair salon on the premises?

6. How often are their rooms cleaned, once a week or twice a week? Is the room checked for trash and cleanliness each day?

7. How often is the laundry done? Does the community wash, dry, fold, and put away the clothes for your parents?

8. Do they have assigned seating in the dining room? Can the kitchen staff handle special dietary needs?

9. How do staff and residents interact. Do the residents seem withdrawn or depressed? Do the staff treat them with dignity?

10. If one partner has dementia, what will happen to the other? Will you try to room them together? After being roommates for many years, they typically will not do well if separated.

11. Do they have a memory care area? Are they allowed to have visitors? Will you, as a visitor, be able to have the code to enter the memory care unit? If not, are they always there to allow you into the unit? Dr. Fagan had one ALF where he visited a patient in the memory care unit. During the COVID pandemic, the facility was very short-staffed. It took him 20-30 minutes to exit the Alzheimer's unit. He was essentially locked inside until somebody could come down and open the door for him. Due to this ALF belonging to a parent corporation it was bound by Corporate policy.

12. Does the community offer in-house and off-property activities? What are the charges? How is that handled? Is there an account for depositing monies, or will a credit card or cash be required?

13. What happens when a parent becomes ill? Does the facility have a visiting doctor? Will they have 911 responders come to the community and transport the sick person to the hospital? How are doctor visits arranged? Will someone take your parents to the doctor or for lab tests? Is there an additional charge for this?

14. How is medication handled? Do you have to have it delivered to the resident nurse, or do they use a local

pharmacy? Do they dispense the medication as needed to the resident? Is there Registered Nurse or Pharmacy Tech on staff?

15. Ask if all the staff members have had background checks. Some states require background checks, but some don't. Ask if the facility is bonded, licensed, and insured. If you doubt their answer, ask to see a copy of the paperwork. If they refuse to show it to you, you may wish to look at another ALF. Remember, these are your parents who will be cared for daily by someone other than a family member. You want to ensure their care and well-being at all times.

16. Ask if management is physically there on the weekends. Unfortunately, the weekends are when staff may or may not be supervised efficiently, and things can fall between the cracks.

17. If your parents attend a house of worship, who will take them to services?

It is important to ask to see the state licensing inspection survey. All facilities will have some deficiencies but if they hand you a 20 page report with deficiencies containing patient care, it is probably a facility to be avoided.

When your parents have been in the community for several years, they will eventually require higher levels of care. Rising costs affect everyone, and assisted living facilities are no different. They may have to raise the rent each year. Are you, your parents, or your siblings prepared for these price increases? Will your siblings or friends also be there to help you, the caregiver, with visits and errand running?

THE VILLAGE CONCEPT

A newer type of senior living is called the Village Concept. It's similar to what a senior would get in a retirement community, but they stay in their own homes. Management acts as a liaison or concierge service and does not provide services themselves. The real help comes from other non-disabled village members, younger neighbors, or youth groups doing community services.

CONTINUING CARE RETIREMENT COMMUNITY (CCRC) AND LIFE CARE COMMUNITIES (LCC)

These communities are a hybrid and consist of independent living, assisted living, and skilled nursing, all in one area. Life Care communities must guarantee health care coverage for life, no exceptions. If the resident exhausts all of their funds, they cannot lose their residence. There is a nursing facility on the campus.

These communities are perfect for the older adult who wants to live in one location for the rest of their life and who doesn't want to worry about arranging for future care needs. Most require a large up front "buy in" as a way to have insurance that you will have a future residence as your health declines. They're also good for spouses who wish to stay close to one another even if one requires a higher level of care than the other. They can start living in the independent living section and then relocate to another part of the community if needs for care increase. Check your State's public health sites for State registered facilities.

NURSING HOME/SKILLED NURSING FACILITY

This option is for those seniors who need 24-hour supervised care with meals, activities, and health management. It is predominantly for the elderly with severe or debilitating physical or mental illnesses who cannot care for themselves. These are usually the facilities that take Medicaid. Nursing homes are an option for seniors with limited personal funds because the government may pick up the fees. They are usually more restrictive than Assisted Living Facilities and have shared rooms.

A licensed physician supervises each resident's care, and a licensed nurse is on staff and on the premises. Nursing homes can usually provide active rehabilitative treatments after strokes or surgeries. They have physical and occupational therapists to help. They may or may not have special services for memory care patients.

WHERE DO YOU GO FROM HERE?

If only the answer to "where do we go from here?" was straightforward and uncomplicated. If only all family members unanimously agreed on the next steps, perhaps caregiving and aging would be simpler. There are many emotions at play. It can be challenging to acknowledge and admit to our mortality, much less that of our parents. You may discover one or both of them becoming more emotional. They may even lash out at you. It's not about you. It truly is about them and how they're trying to handle the final years of their life. Going from their own house to a senior living facility is a total mind shift; not all our parents can adapt to these changes quickly—plan for it to be a process that may take several months. Because the change will mean adjustments, you mustn't wait until a crisis to begin your research.

As you consider your decision to move them or keep them home, one additional point to ponder is about the relinquishment of your caregiver control. Facilities will have rules to keep all residents safe, but it may be restrictive to you and your family members. This was very apparent during the COVID pandemic of 2020 when our elderly nursing home residents were essentially required to be locked down. Of course, this is understandable in light of the medical crisis that swept through the world, but the point is that individual families lost control of their parents' care. One family member whose parent resided in an upscale assisted living facility reflected to Jeanine that she was forbidden from seeing her dad for 6 months. When she finally saw him, his hair had grown so long it reached his shoulders in long grey unkempt strands and his finger nails were 2 inches long. She was shocked because the fees were maintained throughout the lock down. It is not a question of right or wrong, it is a question of how much control can you give up regarding your parents' care? If you have decided to consider moving your parents to a facility, you want to get it right the first time.

It's very upsetting to move a parent into a facility and realize a few months later that this was the wrong community. Again, take your time and start looking at different communities before you get into a serious, we-need-to-move-you-now scenario.

There are two reasons your parents would need to move into a community. First, your parents' care needs become too great to deal with at home because they require specialized equipment or supervision. The second reason is they need access to care 24/7.

Sometimes this is because an injury or illness that sent them to the hospital. Hospital discharge planners and case managers, must ensure that patients are suited to their living conditions before allowing them to go home. If the hospital does not discharge them to their home or your house because they need additional care, you may be forced to consider moving them to another living situation. If the hospital and treating doctors recommend a facility, it is so the patient can receive additional Medicare services. Such services might include IV antibiotics, or physical or occupational therapy. Medicare limits this to less than 30 days.

HOW TO FIND THE RIGHT PLACE

Do your parents have friends who are currently living in a senior-only complex? Do they want to stay in their hometown, or do they want to live near a family member? Ask friends for recommendations. Touch base with their doctor, who may be able to suggest a place. If they are religious, does their church have a community where they can live?

If you use an agency to locate the perfect place for your parents, be aware that websites and companies offering assistance with location services often refer only to those places that have agreed to pay them a fee. Agencies are popular and may help you narrow down the choices, but you should ask critical questions to ensure you're getting the agency with your best interests in mind.

Often placement agencies will preselect options to show you based on which facilities will pay them. If they narrow your choices to only those that will pay their fee, it will dramatically skew what they will show you.

Be sure you ask:

1. How much is the agency paid? Some larger national
   agencies charge the facilities up to 2 months' rent as their
   referral fee paid by the home. Many smaller board and care

homes operate on tight budgets, and sometimes they can't afford these fees. You may miss out on some great smaller housing locations because the referring agency does not present it as an option.

2. How do they get paid? Who is paying for their agency's placement service?

3. Will the agency only place residents in facilities where they have contracts? Most agents only show you to those that have agreed to their rates.

4. Has the agent visited the home or facility they are showing you? Have them tell you when they last visited and what their assessments were at that time.

5. Will the agent meet your loved one to assess their individual personality? If your loved one is still mentally active, you probably don't want to place them in a home where there are mostly demented residents.

6. Will this agent join you in visiting the homes if that is your preference? You may want to see places without the agent so that you can ask your questions.

7. Is the agency paid a flat fee or a percentage commission?

8. How fast will the agency work to help you find a place?

9. As the placing caregiver, are you allowed to consult with more than one senior placement agency, or do you have to commit only to one? Like real estate agents, this is their livelihood. Although they may not want you to consult other agents, you are free to do research and get suggestions from different sources, unless you have signed a contract prohibiting you from doing so. After all, you want to move your loved one into the right facility on the first go around.

These questions will not only help you be more informed, but they'll also help you understand what factors influence an agency's decision to place your loved one in a particular facility.

HOW MUCH CARE DO YOUR PARENTS NEED?

Before making any decisions, it's necessary to determine how much help your loved one needs. Compare that to what you can provide with the help to which you have access. Also, be realistic about how much support the family will provide.

Make a list of everything your senior needs help with on a daily, weekly, and monthly basis. Seeing the whole picture enables you to choose the correct level of care. Be very realistic about how much help you, your family, friends, and neighbors can provide. It would help if you thought about this in terms of long-term, ongoing assistance – a few weeks or months isn't enough.

Once you have compared those two lists, you'll have a better sense of the tasks your older adult will need additional help to accomplish. After looking at the lists and comparing them, you may discover that in-home care may work best; in other cases, Assisted Living may be the better choice.

UNDERSTAND THE KEY DIFFERENCES BETWEEN IN-HOME CARE AND ASSISTED LIVING

Before deciding between in-home care and assisted living, you should consider some key differences.

In-Home Care: Pros and Cons

A caregiver is hired to come into the home and help the senior with daily living activities. In-home care enables your loved one to continue to live safely at home.

The specific help provided depends on your parent's needs. It might include meal preparation, getting around the home, transportation, bathing, dressing, using the toilet, etc.

Pros:

- Your senior receives one-on-one care tailored to their specific needs and preferences.
- Your senior can stay in their own or a relative's home as they age.

71

- Costs can be lower depending on times care will be provided and the caregiver's skill level.
- The family gets to choose the caregiver.
- Your parent gets to know one caregiver rather than being cared for by many different people.
- Various caregiving sources may help reduce overall costs, increase social interaction, or medical-type care.

Cons:

- It can be costly if 24/7 care is needed.
- Family involvement is necessary for hiring and managing caregivers and planning backup care options.
- There is potential for social isolation, which can contribute to depression, cognitive decline, or other health problems.
- The home may need modifications for safety or wheelchair accessibility.
- Housekeeping and home maintenance often needs to be done.
- Groceries, personal care, and household supplies need to be purchased.

Assisted Living: Pros and Cons
Pros

- ALFs offer a wide range of care options.
- Meals, transportation, group activities, and housekeeping are standard at most facilities
- Assisted living might be an affordable way to get 24/7 supervision and care.
- The family can focus more on the relationship with their parents rather than on their care needs.
- The parent has more opportunities for social interaction with other residents.

- The family won't need the added burden of finding and managing caregivers.
- The level of care can be increased as needed because the staff is already in place.

Cons

- One-on-one care might not be as personal or consistent as at home.
- Frequent changes in the care team are common.
- The quality of care can vary depending on the team.
- If significant one-on-one supervision is needed, hiring (and paying out-of-pocket for) private aid may become necessary.
- Some ALFs will not allow a non-employee to come in and take care of the resident.
- Residents can be asked to move for several reasons with little advanced notice.
- If your loved one needs more services, the prices can increase dramatically.
- Your parent may not enjoy living in a group environment.

UNDERSTAND THE FINANCIAL SITUATION

Before choosing for your loved ones, you need to know how each choice will affect and work with their budget. Figuring out the costs is not easy, and it is specific to each person's needs, location, and how much you can expect from a supportive family. Gathering information and analyzing options will take some work, but it will be beneficial as you plan for the future. It avoids unpleasant scenarios, such as your parent suddenly running out of money.

Estimating financial obligations can be complicated, but with a little investigating, you should be able to get a good baseline. After you check on all available payment resources (such as Medicaid, long-term care policies, and medical plans), call for pricing information from several independent or assisted living communities. Compare this to the pricing from several different in-home care providers. You may want to consult an Elder Law Attorney to learn if there are ways to help your parents become eligible for Medicaid.

Once you have these figures, you'll have a reasonable estimate for the costs associated with your parent's needs. There are a lot of factors to consider in making 5 to 10-year financial estimates. If this task becomes overwhelming, you may want to hire a Certified Senior advisor, an accountant, a financial adviser, or a trusted friend to help calculate these numbers. You will want to determine monthly care costs by including the following expenses.

Monthly In-Home Care Costs

1. Hours of care needed x the caregiver's hourly rate
2. Groceries and meal preparation
3. Personal care supplies
4. Household supplies
5. Housekeeping and laundry
6. Transportation
7. Rent or mortgage and property taxes
8. Home and yard maintenance
9. Utilities, water, and garbage

Assisted Living Costs

1. Move-in fee
2. The activity fee is often a one-time charge at move-in
3. The monthly base rates
4. Additional fees for increased levels of care
5. Housekeeping and laundry – are usually included, but if you need extra services, there may be a cost
6. Personal care supplies may be a family responsibility
7. Meals, in-room dining, or snacks
8. Overnight visitor fees

IS IT TIME FOR ASSISTED LIVING?

Sometimes caring for someone at home becomes unsafe or is just too much for the caregiver. If your older adult behaves aggressively, they may have dementia or Alzheimer's disease. Doctors and caregivers usually first try to treat aggression or agitation with redirection which means changing the subject to something the person usually does not find anxiety provoking. If this fails, medications may be needed to keep the loved one in the particular living situation that is needed. The medications should be the least often and the lowest dose possible. The increased agitation could put the caregivers and others at risk. Moving your loved one to a dedicated memory care unit can relieve emotional stress for all involved. This is sometimes very difficult but often the memory care unit has the least disruptions in a routine which relieves much of the anxiety and agitation. Often people are quite content after the initial adjustment period.

Sometimes care needs have become too intense for safe home care. Most aging adults will decline in health and ability. Regardless of the quality of care, they will continue to age, and illnesses and serious diseases may occur. If your loved one now needs constant supervision and care, moving them to an ALF may be the safest and least stressful option. It's tough for caregivers to handle the stresses of caring for Alzheimer's patients. If your parent is of large stature and develops mobility issues, it will become physically impossible to move them and could put the caregiver at risk.

Frequently attempting to leave the house will increase the risk of the Alzheimers patient getting lost and possibly injured. Often the patient with cognitive decline will try to go for a walk to a once-familiar location. You might be at work, and your parent has decided to go on a walk or a drive.

Sam, a very independent 73-year-old, lost his wife during COVID. They had no children. His siblings said he seemed a little off but could care for himself. After his wife passed, he started acting a little strangely. Then he went missing. They all tried to call him, but no answer. They went to his home, and he and his car were gone. His siblings called the police to report a missing person. A few hours later the police notified the family that Sam had been found. He was 150 miles away when he ran out of gas. He did not know what to do but luckily was discovered before he wandered into the wilderness. Sadly, this type of story is not uncommon, so don't minimize your loved one's dementia.

Sometimes you have no idea that a parent is scheming to escape. Dr. Fagan recalls a well-cared-for Alzheimer's patient. The house was safe, and all parties thought he was content. The daughter went to work and his elderly wife was with him. One day she took her eyes off him for a few minutes, and suddenly he was nowhere to be found.

He had escaped, and because of her mobility issues, she could not catch up to him. Fortunately, she called 911, and the police located him before he was injured or wandered off the main road. These scenarios are all too familiar to law enforcement. We hope you will consider them when you are struggling with whether your senior should be at home or be placed in a fully secure memory care community.

In-home care costs are high. Hiring an in-home caregiver is expensive. As your parent ages, they will need more and more help. The decisions are agonizing. They create a lot of caregiver stress. The pressure can be mentally, emotionally, and physically overwhelming if you are a family member caring for a parent. This stress can seriously affect your health and well-being. When you or a sibling gets to that point, your ability to care for your parent can be significantly diminished: sometimes to the point where you're no longer able to care for them safely. Be aware of this by acknowledging the stress and look for solutions.

WHAT ELSE IS CRITICAL TO KNOW?

Power of Attorney

Your parents' physical care and well-being are just one side of taking care of them. Although these points may be repetitive, it is important enough to mention again. Please work on finding the answers to the following questions.

Who has power of attorney (POA) for each of your parents? The importance of this document cannot be overstated. If your parents do not have a POA, make an appointment today and get it done. If parents are incapacitated, such as in a car accident, stroke, heart attack, or severe fall, they need someone who can make a critical life or death decision on their behalf. If there is only one parent, someone must have a POA, preferably a geographically close family member. Jeanine has seen the elderly suffer because the POA was located out of the country and unreachable. The POA should be easily accessible. A copy of it should be made available to all siblings.

Sharon shared two situations over the past ten years where she literally saved both parents' lives. The first time was when Sharon's dad was in the hospital recovering from surgery. Sharon's mom phoned her, stating she was short of breath. Sharon rushed her mom to the local ER and learned her mother had a bilateral pulmonary embolism. The local hospital wanted to send mom to a hospital that could best address this life-threatening issue. Sharon's father could not decide for his wife because he was in the hospital with his own medical problems. Because Sharon had her mom's POA in her hand, the ER team was allowed to life-flight mom to a hospital that was able to save her life.

Situation number two involved her dad when her mother was in the hospital. Her dad had heart issues and had to be taken to a larger city for a quadruple heart bypass which would not have been allowed in the urgent time frame if there had not been a person with the POA in hand to grant permission.

In one year, both parents were in the hospital thirteen times, with nine of these being life-or-death situations. Without that POA, neither one of her parents would still be living. As mentioned in an earlier chapter, her sisters lived hundreds of miles and hours away from their parents. There simply was not enough time to drive to the small town and make a healthcare decision.

Sometimes it can be challenging for family members to allow the geographically close sibling to be the POA. The parents' lives may be at risk when the POA is not the local caregiver. Carl had this situation occur when his dad suffered a heart attack. Carl was with his father when his dad appeared to have a heart attack. He tried to phone the sister with the POA, but there was no answer.

Dad transported to the hospital via 911 first responders. Sister, who was POA, showed up at the hospital and challenged Carl on dad's wishes. An argument ensued, and Carl was required to concede to his sister, who was the POA. As the more involved adult child, Carl knew the most recent choices his father had expressed. Sister acted upon her own personal beliefs of what she wanted for her father. Dad's wishes were not in her decision-making. Unfortunately, this is not an unusual scenario. Be as proactive as possible for the sake of your loved ones. Talk regularly with siblings about the easiest and most efficient way to respect your parent's last wishes. Put aside your grievances to find common ground for the sake of your loved ones.

Medications

As a healthy person, Linda didn't pay much attention to her parents' doctors, the medications they were taking, what the dosages were, and why they were prescribed UNTIL the first time she had to go to the ER with one of them. She felt helpless when asked what medications her dad was taking, and she had to respond with, "I don't know." It took time for the hospital staff to call the doctors and get the medication information.

Many hospitals and physician offices operate on entirely separate electronic medical record systems. Don't expect the hospital to have your parent's recent medical information.

Resolving never to have that happen again, she created a form with the name of the medication, the dosage amount, how often it was scheduled to be taken, and what it was treating. Halfway down the page, she added doctors' names, specialties, and office locations and numbers.

It is recommended that all caretakers do the same thing. Keep several copies in a binder. To be extra cautious, you may want to keep some copies with you. Put the POA in the binder too.

When family members visit, ensure they know where the binder is stored.

Health Insurance Information

In addition to keeping the medical information in the binder, you must ensure, you have all their insurance information. The best way is to make a photocopy of their Medicare and Medicaid cards along with their supplemental insurance policy card.

Jeanine recommends keeping at least two copies of everything in each folder or binder. Again, preparation is paramount. Preparing before anything happens will eliminate an unbelievable amount of stress for you, and it's always a question of when, not if, something happens. Let's face it; a medical crisis does not occur when you have the time to deal with it stress-free. Having all the above information at your fingertips helps eliminate stress, so you can focus on your parent's medical care and your health. All resources cited are listed in the resources section.

Pay attention to different behaviors or patterns in how parents do things. Could something physically be changing for them? It could be the beginning of dementia or several other medical conditions. If so, have your parents checked out by a physician. Resources are provided on this topic in the next chapter.

CHAPTER 6

Being a health advocate.

MEDICAL CARE FOR YOUR LOVED ONE

Sooner or later, your loved one is going to need medical care. Have you talked openly with your parents regarding their wishes? Use their goals, not yours, when you help them make medical decisions. Sometimes medical professionals trained to solve the health issue may offer suggestions for care that don't align with your parents' wishes. For example, if a surgeon suggests surgery, but you understand the risks and have previously spoken to your loved ones about their wishes, you may be required to help them say "no."

You may be vaguely aware of their doctors, but do you know much about the physicians they have been seeing? Wherever you are on your caregiving journey, it is time to start being proactive with health care. Begin by asking your parents if you can write a few things down. Even if it's only to write down the names and contact information for each doctor and how often your parents go to this doctor. Be mindful that you are not trying to take over but to assist them. Some of you will have parents that have always been very healthy and have not seen a need for a regular doctor. Perhaps you may have parents that go to many different specialists. If you find yourself further along the caregiver journey, then it's probably time to start attending some of the appointments. Below are some things you should start documenting and putting in your care-giver binder mentioned in an earlier chapter.

1. Names, specialties, and contact information of physicians
2. Dates of prior visits
3. Frequency of visits to each specialist
4. Medications prescribed by each physician and dosing schedule
5. Pharmacy where medications are refilled
6. Physicians refill policy. If your loved one takes any narcotic or Schedule 2 medication, there will be required visits before refills can be authorized. You don't want your parent to suffer without needed medicines if they have forgotten to get refills.

When you attend medical appointments with your seniors, take note of the staff and providers. Do your parents connect with this provider, or do they feel dismissed? Medical care can vary greatly even in the same state or country. You can assess the doctor's ability to connect to your seniors, but sometimes the best doctors don't have the best bedside manner. Physicians with the subspecialty in Geriatrics will most likely be accustomed to seniors' personalities. But the bottom line is, can they manage your parents' medical issues? If your parents are happy with the care provided and have no complaints, then your parents are probably OK. Your parent may have been seeing a provider for a long time and have a good relationship.

Be aware that if you begin attending appointments, you should tread lightly. You don't want your parent to feel like you are judging the medical care or provider. If there are questions that you or your parents have for the provider, you may need to join them on their visit. You can ask things like:

1. Do they still need to be on the same medication they are currently on?
2. Does the dosage need to be the same?
3. What is the medication treating?
4. Why was it prescribed in the beginning?
5. What are some long-term effects of the medication?
6. Are they able to stop taking it?

7. What could happen if they stopped taking it?
8. Does it conflict with any of the other medications they are taking?

Many seniors have several doctors for various conditions. As your parents decline, you will need to attend these appointments too. Listen to the physicians and keep notes. Sometimes the best of us forgets what the doctor said.   Listen to your parents' concerns. Do they want to continue going to multiple specialists, or is now a good time to switch to a Family Doctor or Geriatrician? They can often manage issues that specialists have set on course. But the decision to streamline doctors depends on your parents' medical needs. Talk to the primary care doctor about it before canceling doctors.

Have you thought about scheduling all your parents' doctor appointments in one week? Why? Crafted schedules can make the caregiver more organized and eliminate the stress of having appointments spread out over several weeks.

Also, your loved ones may appreciate having their meetings stacked together in one week. While you prefer early morning appointments, as seniors age, they may find it more challenging to get up and be ready for early morning doctor appointments. Ask them which they prefer, morning or afternoon appointments. To avoid emotional stress with your loved one first thing in the morning on early times, try scheduling their appointments in the afternoon.

When scheduling appointments in the afternoon, choose the first time after lunch or the last time available of the day. Why? Because there is virtually no wait time for the first appointment after lunch, and if you choose the last one of the day, you can call mid-afternoon and see how late the appointments are running and adjust your time accordingly. Sometimes a 3:30 p.m. scheduled appointment may be re-adjusted to 4:00 pm or later.

Think of ways to make your life easier during the appointments versus a stressful time with your parent. Parents can be a little anxious or cranky while waiting on the doctor. Their wait time in the examination room can become a little tense if they wait idly for the doctor. One thing that can ease their impatience is to play a YouTube video or music for them. It makes time go by faster. You may wish to reward your parent with an ice cream cone or an early dinner if they decide to take the last appointment of the day. Find a reason to give your loved one something to look forward to.

When a loved one becomes ill or needs additional care, their physician may recommend nursing care. If they have had a hospital stay, the discharge planners may suggest a nursing home or an assisted living home. Here many services, such as Physical or Occupational therapy, can be performed. If they can stay home, be aware that various insurance companies offer products to keep seniors home and not in the hospital or nursing homes. Visiting nurses can deliver hydration and antibiotics. Even PT and OT sometimes go to the house.

Ask the physician what recommendations they have for your seniors. Sometimes their doctor may have other suggestions for care or upcoming care that may need to be considered.

What's the difference between nursing care in the home and an in-home care giver?

What do you do if the time comes that your senior needs more care than what you can provide? If a nurse is needed, the physician must request this service by placing an order to the nursing company of your choice or the one dictated by the health insurance plan. If you are at a place where you need an in-home assistant for non-medical care, you can hire caregivers.

Check into your loved one's insurance coverage. It may pay for a program to help your senior stay healthy and out of the hospital. Some Health Maintenance Organizations (HMOs also called Medicare Advantage plans) are now developing an all-inclusive wellness program. For example, some HMOs cover an exercise program called Silver Sneakers. Get to know your parents' medical insurance agent. Put that information in your binder. Ask the agent questions about your loved ones' policies. They should be familiar with what Medicare offers and with your parents' supplemental policy. You may discover they have a long-term care policy that may pay for assistance with daily activities such as bathing, dressing, and getting in and out of bed.

Long-term care policies are different from supplemental insurance. Long-term care may pay for all or a portion of your loved ones expenses in assisted living, a nursing home, adult day care, or additional nursing needs in your home. Inquire through the particular policy.

Keep in that mind that regular supplemental insurance does not cover long-term care. It can also be difficult to secure long-term care insurance if you already have pre-existing medical conditions or are over 70 years old. Long-term policies tend to be on the expensive side, and the premium may increase every year.

Some HMOs now offer house calls for incapacitated seniors. Since the Covid pandemic, telephone or video visits with their physician or physician assistant may provide a suitable alternative to in-office visits. Note that this type of visit may still require caregiver assistance. The technology is challenging for all ages but may be even more complex for the aging brain. Physicians appreciate you helping your seniors master the computer platform they use before allowing them to go "alone" to these virtual appointments.

Each state offers programs designed to help you care for your parent. Many states are now offering a new "all-inclusive" Medical Plan for low-income seniors. One example now with many locations is called Inno-vAge (PACE). Medicare/Medicaid funds PACE to help seniors age at home. It offers coordinated healthcare, specialty care, medication management, in-home assistance, therapy services, and transportation. Unfortunately, PACE is only for low-income seniors with Medicaid, but with time, more plans are being developed for non-low-income seniors. Their needs are similar, and the goal of keeping them independent and out of the hospital is universal, so don't give up. In time we will see more comprehensive programs being developed. There are programs to assist seniors everywhere. It isn't easy to find them. Start by asking the doctor or medical staff for advice. Think about consulting a certified senior advisor. You will find this on our resources page.

It can be very overwhelming to find programs for what your loved ones need. You may do a lot of research online and make local calls to various groups and organizations. It can take a lot of time initially, but you may end up keeping your loved one in their home for much longer than everyone anticipated, and that's the whole goal.

Some programs available in one state may not be open in another state. Larger cities tend to have more resources available than smaller towns. Even if your parents live in a small town, check the programs in larger cities, because the urban based programs may be offered remotely. They just may be headquartered in the larger cities.

Even if programs in larger cities do not extend to your smaller community, ask what they can recommend. You may find out about other programs you had no idea existed. People are willing to provide information once you explain what you're trying to do to provide for your loved ones. Also, don't forget to check the various apps on your cell phone.

"No Wrong Door" is a new organization by the United States government designed to streamline services and resources available for long-term care. Their initiative is that all people, regardless of age or disability, should be able to live independently, participate in their communities, and have the right to make choices and control their decisions for their lives. Staff act as a liaison to help caregivers navigate all options for their seniors.

Although programs vary by state, be sure to research government programs such as Medicare and Medicaid for additional sources of assistance. If caregiving has you too busy to do research, you should consider hiring a Certified Aging specialist. For a small fee they will help you locate resources and or assist with qualifying your parent for state funded programs.

Some programs that may be available for your parent are Meals on Wheels, which deliver food to the homebound. Many restaurants offer delivery services, and your senior may not have even thought about having quality food delivered to the house once in a while.

Senior transportation is offered in many communities. Your loved one needs to be somewhat mobile, and the transport may be able to take them to doctor appointments at no charge.

There are services available to do errands for the elderly. Also, many places now offer free delivery services for seniors.

Habitat for Humanity offers aging-in-place programs for seniors. If your loved one can no longer upkeep their home, Habitat may provide housing for your parents. Check with your local office as to the details and requirements. Getting your loved one into another home may be easier than you think.

The Veterans Administration offers many programs for ex-military seniors. You'll need to have a veteran social worker assist you. Don't give up if you feel like you're not getting anywhere with the VA. Sometimes the right hand doesn't know what the left hand is doing. Keep making calls. Write down the name of the person you spoke with, the date and the time, and keep track of the phone numbers. Do follow up with them. It's not that they're deliberately not returning phone calls, but they are incredibly overworked. Take the initiative to follow up with them every couple of weeks.

Many caretakers have found the VA will turn someone down three times before providing services. Be persistent.

WHAT ELSE CAN YOU DO TO ENSURE YOUR LOVED ONE'S CARE?

Ask questions, ask lots of questions. One question that often leads to a wealth of information is, "Is there anything I have failed to ask that I should know?" It is incredible how much more information you'll receive from that one question. This question works wonders whether you are asking a medical professional or an organization for more information.

There are a lot of community organizations that can provide you with assistance for your loved one. Rotary or Kiwanis Clubs may offer services for seniors. For example, Rotary may build a needed wheelchair ramp for your loved one.

Be sure to ask the following questions of different organizations:

1. What services do you offer?
2. Is there a fee? If so, how much is it?
3. Will my parents' insurance pay for it?
4. How often can you come to my parents' home?
5. Do you have licensed medical personnel on staff?

6. If I have a problem, how is it addressed?
7. Who else do you recommend I talk to?

Does your parent belong to organizations such as AARP, Moose Lodge, etc., where services and programs are offered to support seniors at home? You can call local offices as well as obtain the information online.

Your parents' house of worship may have groups to assist them with their needs. Some high schools may offer a program. Also, certified nursing programs usually have a clinic or rotation schedule they must complete, and taking care of your loved one may help qualified students fulfill some of their requirements.

Some elder care businesses can provide services to your parent; however, if insurance does not assist with costs, it can become costly. Be sure to ask what their charges are before ordering service.

You may discover other programs available for your loved one. Keep asking questions. Yes, it does take some work, but it can pay huge dividends in your parents' overall care and well-being. There may be free programs available regardless of your parents' income level.

Your area may offer a plethora of services. For example, Florida is a retirement state, and many different services are available to seniors, particularly in the more heavily populated areas. Some of these services may not be available in other states. It does pay to look at some of the more heavily populated states to see what programs are offered there and then check with your state to see if the same programs are available. Make your life as easy as possible when looking for programs.

When speaking with various organizations, document the dates, times, and names of people with whom you spoke. This information can be invaluable if you need to so follow up. Keep all of this information in your care binder. Being organized eliminates stress, and you don't have to rely on your memory alone.

Also, it makes it easier to know what organizations you've already researched. There's nothing worse than realizing you've already called an organization. A helpful hint is to keep the organization names in alphabetical order. It's all about making your life easier by keeping track of everything. Check our Resources section for additional information.

CHAPTER 7

Taking care of the caregiver.

ME OR YOU? PUSH-PULL!

Being a caregiver is very rewarding, but it can also be very stressful. For many caregivers, it provides a sense of love that you're there for loved ones when they need you the most. For some, it is a calling; for others, it is a sense of duty.

In an ideal world, there would be time to ask some questions of yourself before making the decision to be your parents' caregiver. We realize that, in most cases, caregivers can be surprised by their role. However, if you are considering this new calling, you should ask yourself the following questions:

1. **What are my needs and my schedule?** If you work in an office all day and you have to drive your kids back and forth to school, will your parents be okay if they are left home alone all day? Or do they need you to be with them during the day?

2. **What are my personal limits?** If your loved ones need someone to bathe, dress, or go to the restroom with them, is that something you're willing to do? These are extremely personal tasks, particularly with members of the opposite sex, which is why some parents would prefer professional care.

3. **How old are my children?** Are they old enough to help with chores? Will they understand you're taking care of their grandparents?

4. **How's my relationship with my parents?** Unfortunately, not everyone has the best relationship with their parents. If you have had a less-than-desirable relationship, you may want to reconsider having them move in with you or taking care of them full-time in their home. Sometimes the past hurts are too much for you. Other times this just might provide an opportunity for you to mend your relationship. Would it be wonderful if you could take that old suitcase full of resentment and throw it out? This healing might help you for a life time. Only you can decide, but we bet that if you are reading this book, you are probably capable of more than you realize. When you start spending more time with your elderly parents, you may find they are not at all like the memories you painfully carry. Maybe you have a great relationship but you still question yourself. You are very normal. This may be a way for you to give back the love and care they gave you. Only you can make these decisions.

5. **Is your family going to emotionally and physically support you as you become the primary caregiver?** This is a tough one, because you may realize your family doesn't want you to do anything different than what you are currently doing. What do you do then? Depending on the ages of your children, you can explain why you are going to be taking care of their grandparents. This can open a door with your children on why you're doing what you're doing. They may fully engage with their grandparents on a deeper, emotional level once you explain why you're doing it.

If you are the one doing most of the in-home caregiving, family members may not understand the 1001 things you do for a loved one. Here is a partial list of what's involved in caring for elderly parents.

1. You are on-call 24/7

2. You may have to bathe or shower parents
3. You have to ensure bathroom safety for them
4. Vacuum, clean, pickup, and dust the house
5. Prepare meals for them
6. Clean up after the meals
7. Engage in conversation and activities with them
8. Purchase groceries
9. Take them to doctor appointments
10. Run errands
11. Manage household repairs
12. Ensure the bills are paid
13. Do laundry
14. Change the bedroom linens
15. Make sure they're dressed properly

Plus, you might have your own family to take care of, and you may be working a regular job in addition to caring for your loved ones. It's no wonder caregivers can become plagued with feelings of self-doubt, guilt, and burnout.

If you're part of the Sandwich Generation, it can be overwhelming between your own family, your job, and taking care of a parent. How do you take care of yourself if you're the caregiver? First, realize you're not Superman or Superwoman. You can't be all things to all people. If you don't take care of yourself first, you're no good to anyone else. It's not being selfish; it's being self-less. You may need to consciously decide to pay attention to yourself and your needs first. Many times, a caregiver will put themselves and their needs on the back burner while tending to everyone else.

How do you know if you have caregiver stress? According to the Mayo Clinic symptoms of this stress are:

1. Feeling overwhelmed or constantly worried
2. Getting too much or too little sleep
3. Gaining or losing weight
4. Feeling tired all the time

5. Becoming easily irritated or angry
6. Losing interest in things and activities you used to enjoy
7. Frequent headaches, body pain, or other physical problems
8. Feeling sad
9. Not eating balanced, healthy meals
10. Abusing alcohol or drugs that may include prescription medications
11. Suffering from depression

You may realize you're hitting burnout on being a caregiver. It can be very emotionally draining to take care of a loved one in addition to everything else going on in your life.

How do you deal with stress?

Having a strategy in place can definitely be beneficial for handling the emotional and physical demands of taking care of your parents.

The following strategies may be of help to you.

1. **Learn to ask for and accept help.** This is often the biggest challenge faced by caregivers. Do not wait until you are so overwhelmed that you get angry at your family members. You family may not realize you need assistance. They see you as someone who seemingly has it all together. Ask for help and be specific with what you need help with. Ask a family member, friend, or church member to take care of your parent for a couple of hours each week so you can have time to yourself. Ask them to run an errand, pick up groceries, or cook a meal. People are usually happy to help with something when they are given specifics to work with. Don't use the same friends over and over again. Learn to share the love of having others help out.
2. **Focus on what you can provide.** It's easy to get down on ourselves over little things. Remember, you are not perfect.

No one is. You're doing the best you can at any given moment. Focus on what you can do in this particular moment, and then move on.

3. **Do a few different things.** There are always going to be a number of things that have to be done in caring for loved ones in their own home. Make a list of what needs to be done. Prioritize the needs and establish a daily routine. You may want to spend a Saturday morning preparing meals for the next two weeks for your parents. You can make your own version of TV dinners and freeze them for your loved ones. All they have to do is take the meal out of the freezer and microwave it. This frees your time up for more quality time with your own family. Perhaps you have always cooked holiday meals. Have another sibling host the holiday meal or order a pre-cooked dinner from the grocery store or your favorite restaurant. Think of ways to make your life easier while taking care of your senior.

4. **Learn to say "no."** This may be the most difficult challenge for a caregiver to learn. You are not being unkind or mean when you say "no" to parents. Having them call or text you six times a day while you're at home becomes more about their loneliness or wanting to be in control. It also means they don't respect your time or your job. Tell them to only contact you in case of an emergency. The fact they can't find their favorite snack does not mean they should call you each time that happens.

5. **Look for connections.** Reach out to other caregivers to find out what resources may be available in your community. You may discover there are classes to help you. Transportation, meal delivery, or housekeeping services may be available.

6. **Support groups.** Your church and community may have several support groups offering emotional and physical support. Local senior centers usually have caregiver support groups. You may also find some good online support groups

through Facebook/Meta. All you have to do is type in key words such as "caregiver" and several groups will pop up. Of course, live groups will provide a deeper connection and a place to create friendships than an online group. People in support groups understand what you're going through. This journey is difficult enough without suffering undue guilt. Finding and being part of a support group is not a sign of weakness. Let others know what you're going through so they can offer suggestions. Admit you need help in dealing with your loved one.

7. **Seek social support.** Make an effort to stay connected with family and friends who offer nonjudgmental emotional support. If you have a friend who is always giving you advice on how and what to do with your parent, you may want to limit your time with that particular friend. Emotional support while caring for a loved one is hard enough without someone else putting in their "two cents worth", particularly if they have not done what you are doing. Set aside time each week for yourself. Taking a walk with a good friend can be very therapeutic.

8. **Set personal health goals.** Set a plan to get enough hours of sleep, do something physical every day, eat a healthy diet and drink plenty of water. Drinking water can help to eliminate stress. Cut back or eliminate excess caffeine in your daily life. Too much sugar and too much caffeine can dramatically affect your energy level as well as make you a somewhat short-tempered.

9. **Don't isolate yourself.** Isolation can be a very real concern when you're a caregiver. You may feel like the only thing you do is take care of your family in the morning, touch base with your parent, go to work, touch base with your parent at lunchtime, stop by and see your parents for a few minutes after work, perhaps prepare a meal for them, go home, prepare dinner for your family and take care of their needs. It's no wonder you're exhausted. Make time for yourself at

least once a week to do something unrelated to your family or your parent.

10. **See your doctor.** Tell your doctor you're a caregiver and listen to their recommendations on how to best care for yourself. Keep an eye on your blood pressure. As a caregiver, Janna experienced a few months where her blood pressure (BP) was out of control. She had not realized that the pounding headaches were due to stress and high BP. Dr Fagan had her imagine her circulatory system as a hose: a hose that has gotten very hard , brittle and sprung a leak. The pressure had to be released. She did not have to put her parents in a facility, she just had to find a way to help herself. With a medication adjustment, and following useful suggestions she is "all better".

Practical ways to avoid caregiver burnout

1. Give yourself permission to cry. There, we've said it out loud! It is not a sign of weakness to have a good cry when taking care of a loved one. Crying is a great stress reliever. There may be days where you feel like nothing is ever good enough, or that you don't have what it takes to be a good caregiver, or that your siblings don't understand what you're going through, or your family feels like you've put them on the back burner. Regardless of the reason, it is absolutely okay for you to have a good cry.

2. Talk with a friend every day. Friends are there for you when you can't be there for yourself. This is not a pity party or constant whining about your parents. No, this is about you talking with someone who's been there for you in the past.

3. Reduce your caffeine intake. Seriously. Drinking coffee all day long can add to the stress you're already feeling. Drinking five Red Bulls or any other highly caffeinated

drinks is not beneficial either. Caffeine can keep you awake at night, and then you feel out of sorts or hung over the next, then you start the cycle all over again. Break that cycle if you're on it. Yes, you may have several days where you don't feel well or are very sluggish. It takes a few days to get all of that caffeine and sugar out of your system.

4. Try to get enough sleep. Stop watching scary movies or television news an hour before you go to bed at night. You want to re-train your body to start slowing down, so you can go to sleep at night.

5. Take a break every day from your parents. It doesn't have to be long, ten minutes can work wonders, but you do need to take a break from them.

6. Give yourself a reward, a treat, once a month. This is something that you enjoy, perhaps a Blizzard from Dairy Queen or a new shirt or blouse, or go out with friends. Reward yourself; after all, this is work taking care of a loved one, anyway you look at it.

7. Play music in the house. Your parent may enjoy listening to what you like.

8. Learn some relaxation techniques such as meditation.

9. If at all possible, take one to two days off per week. Let your parent know you're around but that you need to take time for yourself. They may want to try to do some things of their own around the house.

10. Consider getting them life-alert buttons to wear when you're not around. If anything happens to them, you're able to get assistance for them.

Respite care

There are going to be times when you need to take a few days or more away from your parents. This may be one of the best things you can do. It may also be a needed break for your loved ones as well. Your parents love you but, chances are, they would like a vacation from you as well. Most communities offer some type of respite care, such as:

- **In-home respite.** Give yourself a recess by having health care aides come to the home. They can provide companionship, nursing services, or both.
- **Adult care centers and programs.** Many ALFs offer some type of respite care. They may offer senior daycare for several hours to several days. Some centers provide care for both older adults and children. This is a wonderful way for the two groups to spend time together.
- **Short-term nursing homes.** Some assisted living homes, memory care homes, and nursing homes accept people needing care for short stays while caregivers are away.

The caregiver who works outside the home

Nearly 60% of caregivers work outside of the home, according to the Mayo Clinic. If you work outside the home and you're a caregiver, you may begin to feel overwhelmed. There may come a time when you need to choose to continue working or spending more time caring for your loved ones. This is a decision you'll need to discuss with your family and also with your siblings.

You may choose to decide to take a leave of absence from your job for a period of time. Employees covered under the federal Family and Medical Leave Act (FMLA) may be able to take up to 12 weeks of unpaid leave a year to care for relatives. You may be able to take four weeks off per quarter rather than all 12 weeks at one time. Ask your human resources office about options for unpaid leave. Some states will pay a small stipend for taking care of your parent. There are programs in Florida that will do this. Check our Resources for additional information.

If your loved ones qualify for Medicaid, some programs may pay you to take care of them rather than having them go to an assisted living facility or nursing home.

Take time for yourself. Remember, total burnout isn't helpful for anyone. This is a process you and your family members are going through. You may be able to enlist your siblings to take turns caring for your parents rather than having all of the care left up to you.

CHAPTER 8

The Final Chapter

LETTING GO WHILE YOU HOLD ON

PALLIATIVE VERSUS HOSPICE

I t's never easy to let a loved one go. What do you do when your parent has been hospitalized, and the discharge planner informs you that it's time to take mom home and place her in hospice? You are suddenly catapulted into an arena for which you are unprepared. Isn't it interesting that we know we are mortal, but when it's time to consider the journey's end, we are shocked? Dr. Fagan talks about a patient he had treated for years. She was approaching her 95th birthday, and her adult children still wanted her to continue active treatments for her cancer. She was miserable, suffering from terrible side effects, and was unhappy, exhausted, and sick. Dr. Fagan introduced the idea of palliative or hospice care. The family was shocked that Dr. Fagan did not support ongoing cancer treatments. He stressed the importance of the family listening to mom's wishes, and with some education, they began to understand the differences.

While the focus is on the patients' needs and quality of life, palliative care is not necessarily for imminent death. It can help seniors live with cancer, AIDS, kidney disease, or the side effects of medical treatments. It doesn't replace other treatments.

Hospice care is for those whose physician predicts they have less than six months to live. It is, however, not limited to 6 months. Suppose one is placed in hospice and, due to God, nature, and possibly the added care from hospice, the person continues to live. In that case, the hospice company will apply to Medicare or the insurance company for an extension of benefits. If the patient is still in decline, it is usually granted. If the patient is doing better, it is often best to terminate hospice and save it for the later stages of life's journey. It's a delicate balance for hospice physicians to assess, but good ethical hospices will do what is best for the patient.

END-OF-LIFE PLANNING, HOSPICE, AND BEREAVEMENT INFORMATION

You can help your loved ones by allowing them to plan for their transition. Listening to what the patients want is critical. Being prepared to stick with the wishes of your loved one is paramount. Families can accomplish this by addressing the topic earlier rather than later. If you wait, parents may lose both physical and mental strength to make their own decisions.

Aging With Dignity

The organization called Aging With Dignity provides many resources to help you as the caregiver. They maintain that every person has the right to age with dignity. Because of the organization's core value of belief in God, "Aging With Dignity" recognizes God as the ultimate decision maker, not the government. All humans have an innate need to love and be loved, especially as they become more dependent on others. Every life is a gift from God, and it has value regardless of sickness or age.

Death is not just a medical moment but a personal, spiritual, and emotional time. It will touch you and cause grief and pain, but acknowledging it and empowering yourself and other caregivers with tools will allow some rays of light in on the dark days.

Aging With Dignity has created an easy-to-understand and easy-to-use document called the Five Wishes, Living Will. It's legally valid in nearly every state and meets the legal requirements in 35 states. As of we are unsure how other countries legally view the

¿Info

gInfo is another free resource that assist all caregivers before a crisis occurs. This group has information and state-specific documents to consult for your individual needs. The goal mirrors Aging with Dignity as a means of helping individuals and families learn about, prepare for and find support during the last months of life. CaringInfo was created by the National Hospice and Palliative Care Organization (NHPCO). The website for CaringInfo offers information about:

- advance care planning
- caregiver support
- hospice and palliative Care
- grief and bereavement support

U.S. Department of Health and Human Services offers long-term care information for planning for end-of-life care and financing, including public and private funding.

WHEN IS IT TIME TO LOOK INTO HOSPICE SERVICES?

If your loved one is not benefiting from active treatment and a cure is no longer possible, it is time for hospice. Hospice will provide care and medical treatment to enhance the quality of life. Hospice care aims to allow the patient to live the final months, weeks, days, or hours in the most comfortable, pain-free environment possible. Hospice does not take over caregiving but will educate and provide emotional support for caregivers and family members. The hospice team will lead the care of your loved one. This team functions together under the guidance of the hospice physician.

When you decide on hospice, ask your parent's personal doctor if he/she will continue following your parent through death. Primary care doctors do not have to be part of the team, but some physicians are willing to work alongside the hospice team. In addition to the medical care team members, clergy, social workers, and trained volunteers help your loved one.

The nurses will regularly visit and, under the supervision of hospice doctors, provide pain and symptom medications and management. Care-aides will assist the caregivers with bathing the patient. They will provide all of the durable medical equipment needed for comfort care. This equipment might be a hospital bed, bedside table, commode, wheelchair, and even supportive floor cushion pads if there is a risk of the patient rolling out of bed. Nurses and doctors will educate the patient and caregivers on what to expect as the patient gets closer to the end of their journey. Hospice should provide 24/7 call support.

Preparing for the end of life can be very frightening to families. Is it too soon to start hospice? Is it too late to start hospice? Barbara Karnes, the award-winning end-of-life educator, suggests calling hospice as soon as your parent or loved one is getting weaker despite treatment, or when the caregivers have difficulty coping with your life-threatening illness. Don't wait. You and your family deserve this support as you help your loved one transition from this life to the next.

Your town or city may have several hospice companies for you to evaluate. We encourage you to evaluate them before making last-minute decisions since hospice is the final place for your loved one. You will want to feel a good connection to the hospice company. You can ask friends in the area about the hospice companies they may have had experience with, or you can ask your loved one's treating physician. Another resource is National Hospice Locator, a free website service showing hospice companies in your local community. It allows you to put in your zip code and other parameters to sort for one that meets your needs. Call the recommended hospices and arrange for a representative to meet with you. The National Hospice and Palliative Care Organization also has a website to locate hospices in your area and has created a worksheet to guide you as you interview various hospices.

NHPCO suggests you ask the following questions when choosing a hospice:

1. What kind of services are provided?

2. What kind of support is available to the family/inner circle/caregiver?
3. What roles do my physician and the hospice physician play?
4. What does the hospice volunteer do?
5. What does the hospice do to keep the patient comfortable?
6. Are services provided after hours?
7. How and where does hospice provide short-term inpatient respite care?
8. Which nursing homes or long-term care facilities does your hospice work with?
9. What is the time frame for hospice to enroll someone once the service request is made?
10. How is payment covered?

To begin any hospice service, the referring doctor must send a referral directly to the hospice. This referral will include some information about your parent's medical condition. The hospice physician is the one who has the authority to determine whether or not the patient fulfills the Medicare or Insurance plan required parameters for hospice benefits. Your hospice representative will need your loved one's Medicare card identification and social security number to make that decision. Please keep these in your binder.

When you request a hospice referral from your primary care office, stress the urgency of this request. You don't want your request to be in a medical queue. It needs to be at the top of the work pile so that the hospice company can make the necessary arrangements to begin service as soon as possible. Be pushy if you need to be. There have been times when medical offices were short-staffed and did not process the referral for hospice until after the patient died. Don't let that happen to your loved one. After the referral is sent to the hospice company and it is determined that the patient is eligible, the hospice company will send a representative to gather the needed signatures and begin services immediately.

As your parent enters the last leg of the journey, we suggest you have conversations about final wishes.

CHAPTER 9

Preparing your loved one and yourself for the inevitable:

GETTING READY TO SAY GOODBYE

We prepare for our children's births, so we must prepare for the death of our parents. When the baby leaves the comfort of the womb, it has gone from one world to another. Like birth, death is leaving this world to be born into the next. Being prepared ahead will prevent chaos from happening at the moment of departure. We have created the following list of items you may want to discuss with your aging parents. Some of these will be easy but some may be too much for your parent. You know your parents best, so respect how they feel when you ask them questions about their wishes. Write it all down and include it in the binder.

1. Create a list of family and friends that you want to notify upon death of your parent.
2. How will you pay for the funeral?
3. Select a funeral home.
4. Do they want cremation or burial?
5. If burial is planned, where will they be buried?
6. Select casket or urn.
7. Where will the funeral service be held and who will preside?
8. Are they eligible for a military funeral?
9. What kind of flowers or music do they want?

10. Do you want a celebration of life?
11. Where will this celebration be held?
12. Who will handle the details of this celebration?

Thinking about these questions ahead of time will help you maintain a calm spirit after your loved one has passed. Churches often have ministries that will help with planning and serving guests at memorial celebrations. Funeral homes also will be very knowledgeable about what needs to be accomplished to honor and celebrate your loved one.

As Annie's mom aged, many of her friends began passing away. Annie often chauffeured her mom to the funerals of her friends. As they drove home, they used the time to talk about the service. What did they like or not like about the funeral? Was the music meaningful? Was the reception nice with delicious food? By the time Annie's mom passed away, her daughter knew exactly what her mom wanted at her final celebration of life. In fact, her mom had pre-selected the bible readings, music, and even the food that would be served. Knowing exactly what their mom wished was a help to soften the sadness as they said goodbye.

If your parent is ex-military, there are burial benefits. Those who qualify for burial benefits include veterans who have served active duty. The National cemetery burial will consist of opening and closing the grave, a headstone or marker, and perpetual care of that area. Be sure to tell the funeral director if your loved one was a veteran.

Certain National Oceanic and Atmospheric Administration (NOAA) and Public Health Service (PHS) officers and WWII Merchant Mariners are also eligible. Tell the funeral home about your parent's involvement with any military branch. This is a beautiful benefit that our military deserve.

Death is not easy for our humanness to manage. Most of us have not witnessed death. It's frightening, mysterious, sad, and something we hope never happens to our parents or loved ones. But we know we can't stop it.

Remember, you can do this! You can stay by your loved one through the end of their journey. Accept that you don't need to "do" anything at this time. You just need to be there in support. Most caregivers are so used to giving care that it's challenging to stop doing something. But friends, you can now rest and let your love one rest. Just be there. Don't be afraid. Understand that for most people dying is a transition to a deep sleep. Breathing slows, and the person doesn't wake up.

THE DYING PROCESS

Most people are not aware of the physical aspects of the dying process. There are some signs of approaching death. Not all will go through this process with the same exact timing, but most fall into the following stages.

A few months before the end, your loved one may be less hungry and thirsty. Nothing seems to taste as good anymore, and the body starts to lose weight. It is okay for the dying to eat less. The body does not need as much energy from food or hydration anymore. Many family members are concerned when their loved ones have decreased fluid intake. Often they ask about IV hydration. It has been shown that giving IV hydration to a dying patient causes the fluid just to leak into spaces it shouldn't go like the lungs and soft tissues, causing shortness of breath and swelling. The fluid does not stay in blood vessels to prevent dehydration.

As sleep increases, the patient may be in and out of this world, preparing for the next. "That requires more spiritual energy," states Barbara Karnes.

As they sleep a few weeks before death, you may hear patients having conversations with others. They might see deceased relatives in the room when they are awake or talk to them while asleep. The Irish often talk about the ancient Celtic spiritual belief that our the dying are very close to the other world. It is referred to as being in the "Thin Space". The Thin Space between this life and the next is only divided by a veil. Perhaps saints, angels, and ancestors are introducing your loved one to the new world. Stay confident that something wonderful is happening. You will notice a change in body temperature that can go between hot and cold. The skin will be flushed. The hands and feet will be old due to the slowing blood flow, and the nails will become slightly blue.

Sometimes the dying get anxious, and your presence can be calming. You may see them moving their arms or picking at things. The breathing can increase and then decrease.

As parting gets closer, within hours or minutes, the blood pressure will drop. The heartbeat becomes weaker and harder to feel. The heart rate will increase to 120-140 beats per minute. Breathing may be more congested, and you might hear gurgling sounds. There may be wetting and even bowel movements while the patient sleeps. The patient may be sleeping with their mouth partly open, which can cause the mouth to get dry. Use some water-moistened swabs to wipe the inside of the cheeks and the lips. Don't put water in the mouth if the patient is non-responsive.

It's essential to provide pain treatment through the dying process. Pain and anxiety increase as the body shuts down. Reposition the body if there is no pain but don't move the patient if it hurts. Moving the person will help decrease bed sores that could arise from the breakdown of the skin.

At this time, your loved one is working hard to let go. Your loving, kind words and permission to leave you will be soothing and calming. Patients can hear and understand your comments, so don't talk about them in their presence. This is a good time to invite a Priest, Rabbi, Chaplain, Minister to bless your parent. The dying can be relieved of anxiety when they experience prayer. You may want to pray out loud or silently as you accompany your loved one. Reassure the dying of your love and appreciation and forgive them for the any hurts they may have caused.

A few minutes before death, their breathing might be "fish mouthed" or open pursed lips like a fish as they breath. Breathing will be slow at 6-8 breaths per minute. The patient may grimace, or even move suddenly. There should be medications easily available for pain, anxiety and shortness of breath. Sometimes the dying may sit up. Don't be alarmed. Stand near the patients' head and gently rest your fingers on their neck to feel for a pulse. You may feel the body release as it crosses over. When there is no breathing for a few moments, your loved one has crossed over.

Allow those that have gathered to share a moment of silence and grief. This is not easy. It is final and all of you will need time to process the event. After death has occurred, you may want to wipe your loved one's body. Family may find this final act of love comforting.

Do not call 911. As we previously stated if you call 911 and paramedics arrive, they will have to do CPR unless you have a signed POLST or DNR. States vary on the requirements of reporting a death. If your loved one is receiving hospice services, the hospice company will know the protocol. Call the hospice company. If the patient is not on hospice you will need to call a funeral home, or non-emergency police number. They will instruct you on your State's requirements. Some States allow for the funeral home to come and pick up the body, but other states may require a coroner. We advise you to look into this prior to your loved one's death.

After you have said goodbye, it's time to revisit the final wishes of your parent.

GRIEF IS PART OF LETTING GO

Grief is a natural part of death and can appear at the oddest times. Some people show little to no emotion at the passing of a loved one. Tom, who lost his mom six months ago, said he was driving down the street when a wave of sadness swept over him. Tom was so overcome with grief that, he had to pull over and let it flow out of his broken heart. That is part of healing after loss. Honor yourself by acknowledging your feelings.

The five stages of grief, as identified by Elizabeth Kubler Ross are: denial, anger, bargaining, depression, and acceptance.

Denial can come in many forms such as thinking your loved one is in the next room or has gone on vacation. Perhaps there is total disbelief.

Anger might bubble up against your departed parent. This can happen if you still have unresolved issues with the things parents may have done or may have failed to do. You may be angry at yourself for things you did or did not do.

Bargaining is when we start to make deals with ourselves or God. It is an attempt to feel better and remove the pain of loss. It can be the overwhelming thought of "what if I had done this or that differently, would my loved one be here today?"

Depression can arise due to a sense of profound loss. Even though you rationally knew your parents were mortal, you now have to create a life that does not include them. This depression can take a month or even years to overcome.

Acceptance comes when you are at peace with the knowledge that your loved one continues in your memory and is imprinted upon your heart.

TAKING CARE OF YOURSELF AFTER A LOVED ONE HAS DIED

Grief is different for each of us. Give yourself time to grieve. Forgive yourself for the things you wish you had done or wish you had said while they were alive. Focus on ways to be kind to yourself. This may be having fresh flowers in your home. It may be a particular song or music that nurtures you.

Allow yourself to feel your feelings. You may want to journal your thoughts. There is no right or wrong way to grieve.

Talk to a trusted friend or therapist about your feelings. Listen to your body. You may want hugs from friends or wish to have time alone. Honor that by telling others what you need. Friends can feel uncomfortable with your parent's death. They don't know how to react. Letting them know helps both of you.

Find a reason to laugh every day. Laughing does not mean the grief is gone, but it provides some good brain chemicals to decrease your sadness. Watch a YouTube video or a funny TV show. Even if you have to force yourself to laugh, it will make grieving a little easier.

When your loved ones have passed, you may not know what to do with the extra time. Do something different. Light a candle, dip your hands in a running stream and smell the aroma of food cooking in your neighborhood. Do something that involves sight, smell, hearing, touch, and taste. Using all five senses, to take in the things around you, will help you be more present in your life.

Change up your daily routine. Perhaps you take time to journal every morning for a few minutes or take a quick walk before or after work. Turn on the radio and get groovy. Yes, that means dancing by yourself or with a friend. That's right, even if you don't have a sense of rhythm, dance movements will help your body relax. Perhaps you will even laugh out loud.

Learn different breathing techniques. You don't have to sit in uncomfortable positions for long periods to do this. You can sit in a chair or lie on your bed and inhale to the count of 4; exhale to the count of 5. This breathing technique will reduce your stress level.

Do something every day that makes you feel good. You might treat yourself by watching a beautiful sunrise with cup of coffee or going for a walk alone. Honor yourself for the time you gave to your loved one. Love yourself in the moments you are overcome with loss. Remind yourself that you did the best you could.

Personal hygiene still matters when you're grieving. Rather than hiding in a dark room or house and not bathing for several days, take a shower or a luxurious bath.

Open the shades and the blinds, and let the light brighten your darkness. Open a window or door and let fresh air into your house. Fresh air can clear out old feelings.

Grieve however you need to, but don't overlook ways to honor yourself, your feelings, and what you're going through. Grief does not have a set of rules nor a clock. It can take days, weeks, and even months before the pain subsides. That's okay. Be gentle with yourself. Family members may cope with their grief differently than you do. It's okay. For a caregiver, the pain of loss may be infinitely deeper than a sibling who only came to visit once a month. Honor others in the way they need to grieve while at the same time letting them know what you need for yourself.

It is normal for variable times of grieving, but the sever and prolonged grief may be abnormal. As a general rule, if you are still functioning and getting up every day to do things you need to do as well as looking forward to doing things you enjoy, it falls in to the category of normal grieving. If, however, you are preoccupied with thoughts and memories of the deceased to the point the you have trouble functioning, you may have prolonged grief disorder. If you feel like crying every day and have lost interest in things you usually enjoy, then you may be suffering from a major depressive disorder. The latter two conditions above should be addressed with counseling and/or medication.

Conclusion

"You Must Take Your Place in the Circle of Life"
The Lion King

As you can see, becoming a caregiver to our parents can be a beautiful part of our journey. Being prepared is critical to creating a place where your parents, your family and you thrive. Caregiving to your parents' is something that will continue to contribute to your family and the culture long after your parents have passed. It is a matrix that holds families together. Strong families build strong communities and strong communities contribute to a strong nation. We want our nation to sustain, therefore we must continue to nurture the family unit. We applaud you for your willingness to contribute to the care of others.

It is hoped that the knowledge you gained while reading this book has helped you prepare, organize, understand, gain empathy, and believe in your ability to care and to give. Today is a good day to create the suggested binder. You will find organizational suggestions in the resources section and the various resources cited. By approaching this part of life with the belief in your ability to do the right things, you will experience the joy only a caregiver can feel. A wise friend once shared the thought that you will never regret giving too much time to the care of your parents. However, you may regret it if you think you have not done enough for them.

Remember Sharon's mom, who nearly burned her house down? A few years ago Sharon persuaded her to write Love Letters to each of her children and grandchildren. She suggests you do the same. As of this writing, she is still receiving Sharon's caregiving skills. She's now 95 years old and as feisty as ever, so please listen to her recommendations.

End-Book Review Page

Caring for the Carers

As you prepare your binder and get ready to embark on this important next chapter, you might want to reach out a helping hand to other people in your situation.

Simply by leaving your honest opinion of this book on Amazon, you'll show new readers where they can find all the guidance they need to approach caregiving with confidence and compassion.

Thank you so much for your support. Our parents aren't the only ones who need us – we need each other too.

PLEASE REVIEW HERE
1. **Click on hyperlink**
2. **Click on review**
3. **Or scan QR code**

The Caregivers Binder

Your parents wishes:

1. Who do I want to make decisions for me when I can't
2. What kind of Medical Treatment do I want or not want
3. When I am dying how comfortable do I want to be
4. How do I want people to treat me
5. What I want my loved ones to know

Legal documents

- Power of Attorney
- POA for financial
- POA for Health care (decision maker)
- Advanced Directives or Living will
- POLST
- DNR
- Copies of Medicare, Medicaid, and Social Security Card

Logistics

Will or Trust- where are they located in your home
Where are titles for vehicles, boats, etc stored

oney

1. All accounts at all banks: who are on the accounts?
2. Investments
3. Insurance
4. Photocopies of Credit Cards
5. Bills: How are they paid and which accounts are they paid from

Medical

1. Doctor name and address
2. List of medicines and who prescribes them
3. What medical problem is each medication supposed to treat
4. Pharmacy: Phone numbers and locations.

After Arrangements

1. Are there pre-paid arrangements
2. Where will services be held
3. Who should be notified

Notes and journaling

Resources

Genworth.com/aging

FiveWishes.org

TheConversationProject.org

Medicare.gov

Medicaid.gov

Veterans Health Administration - va.org

Administration for Community Living - https://acl.gov/programs/connecting-people-services/aging-and-disability-resource-centers-programno-wrong-door

Centers for Independent Living - https://acl.gov/programs/aging-and-disability-networks/centers-independent-living

State Health Insurance Program - https://acl.gov/programs/connecting-people-services/state-health-insurance-assistance-program-ship

Eldercare Locator - https://eldercare.acl.gov/Public/Resources/Topic/Caregiver.aspx

Senior Housing Options - https://dailycaring.com/senior-housing-options-overview/

InnovAge.com

No Wrong Door - https://nwd.acl.gov/index.html

Veterans Services - https://nwd.acl.gov/serving-veterans.html

PACE - https://www.npaonline.org/pace-you/pacefinder-find-pace-program-your-neighborhood#:~:text=Currently%2C%20147%20-PACE%20programs%20operate,click%20on%20your%20state%20below.

Habitat for Humanity Habitat.org. https://www.habitat.org

HealthFinder.gov. Https://healthfinder.gov

VA Caregiver - https://www.caregiver.va.gov/index.asp

AARP Caregiving - https://www.aarp.org/home-family/caregiving/

Alzheimer's Association – alz.org

ARCH - National Respite Network - https://archrespite.org/respitelocator

Family Caregiver Alliance - https://www.caregiver.org/

GrandFamilies.org

Caregiver Action Network – caregiveraction.org

Caregiver- https://www.caregiver.org/

AgingwithDignity.org

Find a Caregiver - https://www.nhpco.org/find-a-care-provider/

Hospice – NHPCO.org

Hospice Finder - https://www.caringinfo.org/types-of-care/hospice-care/choosing-and-finding-hospice-care/

Hospice Foundation of America – HospiceFoundation.org

CompassionateFriends.org

Longtermcare.gov

Knowledge Reduces Fear (Volume 1) by Barbara Karnes bkboooks.com

On Death and Dying (1969) Elizabeth Kubler-Ross

Gone From My Sight by Barbara Karnes bkbooks.com

The Diagnostic and Statistical Manual of Mental Disorders, fifth edition (DSM 5)

Lion King by Disney

Wight, K. (2022, September 9). 16+ short quotes about caring for aging
parents | Cake blog. Cake: Create a Free End of Life Plan.
https://www.joincake.com/blog/caring-for-elderly-parents-quotes/

About the Authors

John Fagan MD

Dr. Fagan is a Board-Certified Geriatric and Family Physician with over 35 years in private practice. He is the Medical Director of Casa Colina Hospital Senior Evaluation center and Casa Colina's Elher's Danlos/Hyper-mobility Diagnosis and Treatment Center located in Pomona, California. In addition to his private practice at Aspen Family Medicine in Rancho Cucamonga, California, Dr. Fagan is an associate Professor at Riverside Medical School and board member of the Inland Empire Foundation Medical Group.When he's not working, you'll find him on the golf course or at home spending time with family.

Jeanine Fagan MBA

Jeanine retired after 30 years in the pharmaceutical industry. She then found herself called into the field of hospice where she experienced and witnessed the struggles facing many seniors and their families. She currently advocates for seniors and helps her aging parents.

Jeanine and John met at the University of San Diego in "Chemistry" class. Married during John's medical school years and Jeanine's Master of Business Administration program they've survived many study hours and still consider themselves students of life. They have four adult children and reside in California.

Made in United States
Orlando, FL
30 May 2024

47359680R00068